SHARON TATE
RECOLLECTION

Debra Tate

Foreword by Roman Polanski

Contributing Photo Editor – Arieana Tate Mussenden

Running Press
PHILADELPHIA · LONDON

CONTENTS

Photo by Roman Polanski

Foreword

Even after forty years, it is difficult to write about Sharon.

In those days, she was not just the love of my life, she was the love of everyone's life, as you can see by reading the tributes paid by so many people throughout this book.

The book itself is a tribute to Sharon: to her beauty, to her spirit, to her talent, to the pleasure her presence gave to everyone who knew her.

It is impossible, of course, to imagine what might have been if Sharon had lived. But this book allows me to remember what was. There is sadness and joy in those memories but there is also a great depth. To me that depth can best be understood by the photograph on page 263. It captures the Sharon I knew and will always know.

ROMAN POLANSKI
Gstaad, October 16, 2013

Introduction

For many years now I have wanted to write a book about my sister, Sharon Tate, as I felt it was my responsibility to help preserve her considerable photographic legacy. As I looked around I came to realize that her enormous popularity, both as an actress and as a '60s fashion and style icon, was continually growing.

Today she is everywhere. New fan blogs and websites are constantly appearing. People are spotted on the street wearing Sharon Tate T-shirts. Fashion designers, like Julien Macdonald, send their models down the catwalk in hair and makeup inspired by Sharon in *Valley of the Dolls*. Celebrities like Madonna, Sarah Jessica Parker, Lindsay Lohan, Adele, Sharon Stone, Blake Lively, and Jessica Paré from *Mad Men* reference Sharon's style in their public appearances, photo shoots, movies, and television shows. And Drew Barrymore appeared on the cover of *Harper's Bazaar* for a major fashion editorial, in which she attributed her idea for the art direction, hair, and makeup as being a homage to Sharon.

In 1969 my sister was involved in an event that changed the country in ways that still resonate. Through her fame, and the hard work of my family and I, she has become the recognizable face of a cause that continues to save lives to this day. That said, I always felt it was very unfair for her life to be remembered primarily for its final moments.

Sharon had a magnificent life. Born into a family who loved her very much, she had a wonderful childhood. She traveled the world. She became a film star who many say was the most beautiful of her generation. She was talented. She met and married the man of her dreams. She experienced impending motherhood. She achieved so much in such a brief time, made a significant impact, and continues to fascinate and delight the world. It is important that her life be celebrated for these reasons.

The idea for this book was not to present a traditional biography, but to carefully assemble photographs and pair them with recollections from myself, Sharon's friends, costars, work associates, and even Sharon herself. I hope this will provide her legions of current and future fans with a well-rounded sense of who Sharon really was—of the gentle and supremely unique spirit that existed beyond her screen persona.

Today, Sharon remains as big a part of my family as ever. As aunt to my beautiful daughter, Arieana, I constantly see her looking back at me not only in Arieana's face but also in her demeanor and most subtle mannerisms. For this reason, Sharon is never far away.

Sharon was and continues to be my sister, my best friend, and my guiding light. I am extraordinarily proud of her—and I know that she is extraordinarily proud of me.

DEBRA TATE

The American Dream Girl

SELECTIONS FROM THE TATE FAMILY ALBUM

1943–1959

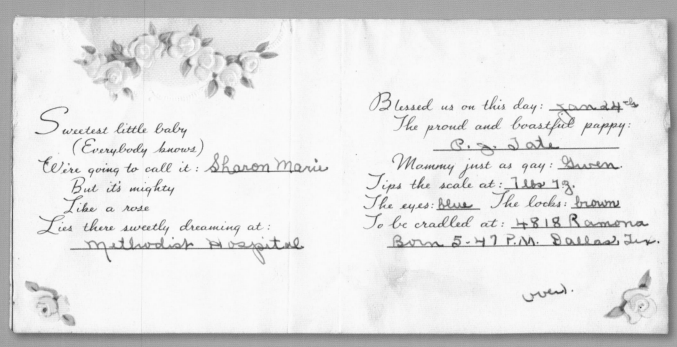

S weetest little baby
  (Everybody knows)
W e're going to call it: Sharon Marie
  But it's mighty
  Like a rose
L ies there sweetly dreaming at:
  Methodist Hospital

B lessed us on this day: Jan 24th
  The proud and boastful pappy:
    P. J. Tate
  Mammy just as gay: Gwen.
J ips the scale at: 7 lbs 7 z.
  The eyes: blue The locks: brown
J o be cradled at: 4818 Ramona
  Born 5.47 P.M. Dallas, Tex.

  (over).

Sharon's birth announcement

Proud dad P.J, with our mother Doris Gwendolyn, shows Sharon off for the first time.

Sharon Marie Tate.
7. mos old.

Dallas, Texas, 1943

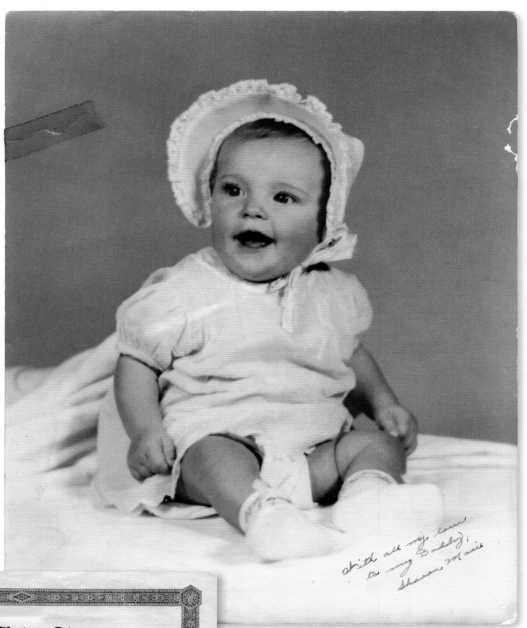

With all my love
to my Daddy,
Sharon Marie

Sharon at 4 months

"I'm sure all new mothers think the same thing, but I truly felt Sharon Marie was the most beautiful baby ever born. All my friends agreed. Knowing my husband Paul would shun such foolishness, I saw an ad in the paper for Miss Tiny Tot of Dallas and without thinking sent a photo of 4-month-old Sharon wearing a white dress and black patent shoes. What can I say, it was a whim. When she won, I admit I was not surprised, but I was afraid Paul would be upset. When he saw the newspaper he beamed and agreed that she did indeed deserve such an honor."

DORIS TATE (Mother)

Sharon (left) and the neighborhood gang displaying their prized
toys. Dallas, Texas, c. 1947

Sharon at age 5

Opposite: Sharon
and Mom, c. 1945

Sharon, 1947

Sharon (second from left) at her First Holy Communion. Houston, Texas, c. 1947.

"When I was in school, I dreamed about becoming a psychiatrist or a ballerina. Like most girls I would dream about becoming a movie star too. But those dreams are the impossible kind, the kind you don't really set your heart on."

SHARON TATE

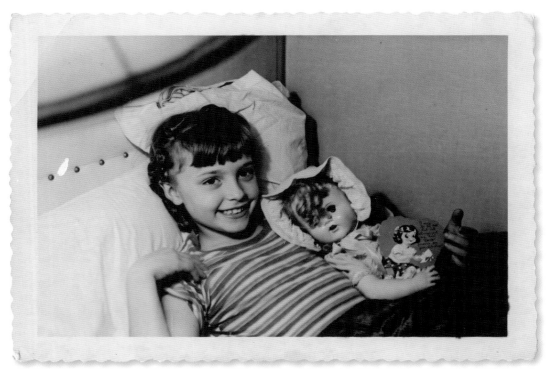

Six-year-old Sharon, Nannie Tate's house, Houston, Texas

Sharon at 6 years, Hot Springs, Arkansas

Opposite: Sharon and "Lady" in PJ's old bedroom at
Nannie Tate's house on Freeman Street in Houston, 1949.

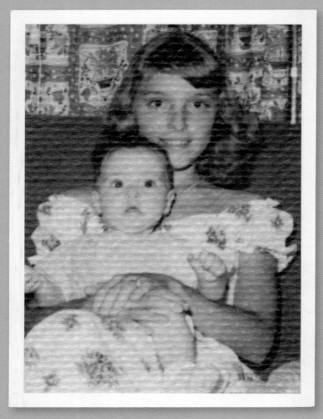

Sharon at 10 years and Debbie at 6 months

4th Grade

6th Grade

Sharon at 13 years

6th Grade, Pasadena, Texas. Sharon is second row, second from the right.

c. 1956

It was September 1955, my eighth grade year at Chief Joseph Junior High School in Richland, Washington. I started noticing a student in the hallway that I hadn't seen before. When I went up to introduce myself she said her name was Sharon Tate. She was in the seventh grade, a year behind me. Sharon said that her dad was in the Army and that the family had been transferred from a base in Texas to Richland. As we parted for classes she smiled with what I would come to know as "Sharon's famous smile." Sharon and I seemed to have an instant friendship. We were always laughing about something—boys, classes, and all the normal things that teenagers talked about. Whenever her name came up, the other students always talked about how pretty and fun she was. Everyone liked her.

One night, a few years later, I picked up Sharon at her parents' home and we drove off heading for George Washington Way. We were chatting when suddenly a dog ran out in front of the car. We heard him yelping. Since it was dark we could hardly see the dog, but quickly got out of the car to start looking. We were both crying. We just knew the dog had died. We searched the alleyway for a while but after about half an hour we gave up, hoping that the dog was still alive. There was a compassion about life in Sharon that I had never seen in another person.

Another memory was visiting the Tate's home. Mr. and Mrs. Tate were always fun to be around—always strict, but in a good way.

You knew where Sharon got her friendliness from when meeting her family. Patti, Sharon's baby sister, was born when I was sixteen and I couldn't wait to see her. Sharon was so proud of her. When I arrived, Debra, Sharon's five-year-old sister was already asleep. Patti was being held by different visitors and my turn to hold her finally came. Sharon was smiling away. Soon Mrs. Tate announced that it was time to feed Patti. She invited the girls into her bedroom while she breast fed Patti explaining that this was "girls' time." Mrs. Tate's motherly ways were always prevalent.

Sharon's popularity grew by leaps and bounds throughout her time in Richland—she went from Princess at the sophomore dance to being crowned Miss Richland. It was so exciting when she won. Sitting there watching her crowned, so full of joy, was delightful. Sadly, her father was transferred to Italy and the family left not long after her crowning. Sharon and I didn't keep in touch when she left Richland. When I heard from other students she was back in the United States acting in *The Beverly Hillbillies* I didn't miss an episode. Sharon was so naturally beautiful that I didn't like seeing her with all the makeup she wore when she was on the show. Then came *Valley of the Dolls* and thankfully she looked more natural. In my heart of hearts I knew Sharon was going to make it as a star.

PATTI JONES AHRENS

Sharon and Debbie in
Washington state, 1957

Sharon at 14 years, Debbie at 5 years.
Galveston Beach, Texas, 1957

27

Sharon at 15

Sharon at the Officer's Club, Richland,
Washington, 1958

Left: Alameda, California, February 13, 1956

Queen of the Autorama, 1959

While we were living in Richland, Washington, Sharon was crowned "Queen of the Autorama." The dress she wore was a bright shade of pumpkin orange. It was a thinly strapped gown, tight at the waist, with a very full skirt. Underneath the skirt were what seemed like a hundred layers of petticoats to help produce that highly desired hourglass figure. In an attempt to avert a fashion disaster, for the crowning ceremony Sharon assigned me "Keeper of the Petticoats." This was perhaps not the best responsibility to give to a six year old with mischief on her mind. My job was to go under the skirt, straighten out the avalanche of tulle, and make sure everything sat just right. Meanwhile, mom and the other girls were busy putting the finishing touches on Sharon's outer dress, hair, and makeup.

"Sis" started to get a little fidgety, so I moved as she moved, a few steps this way or that way. They asked her to "stand up, sit down," over and over and over. All of these requests were to make sure there would be no wardrobe malfunctions when she went out on stage to meet the audience. Suddenly, curled up in a ball under her skirt, I got the harebrained idea that I would be comic relief by grabbing people's ankles or feet as they neared the rim of the dress. This would surely make Sharon smile, I thought to myself. First I started with the other girls competing. Like a kitten hiding under a couch poised for the attack, I would wait for an approaching stiletto, extend my hand, and then quickly grab the unsuspecting ankle. One by one the girls shrieked with shock, laughed, and then continued their task. They caught on very quickly, but even so, the gag worked because Sharon was soon giggling.

I continued a few more times and then Sharon started to poke around with her orange sateen pump, to try and discover my location. She finally succeeded to hook me with her foot, ever so gently, and slide me toward the interior of the skirt. Needless to say, I wiggled free and moved back to the outer layer of the dress to continue my torment. I was having way too much fun from under that skirt to stop.

The next person I grabbed was a man, much to my disappointment. I had his pant leg in my tight little fist. He jumped back and fell on his butt. Very startled, I peeked out from under the dress. Our eyes met just in time for me to see that he had knocked over a card table containing mirrors and other beauty necessities. My head shrunk into my shoulders. I knew I was in big trouble.

As I emerged from my lair, Sharon just smiled at me, offered the man a hand up, and said to him, "I think they want us on stage now." The man picked up the microphone, grabbed Sharon, and off they went through the curtain. Perfect timing—Sis got me out of yet another pickle.

Queen of the Tri-City Autorama, April, 1959

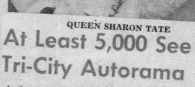

QUEEN SHARON TATE

At Least 5,000 See Tri-City Autorama

Another capacity crowd is expected today for the third and final showing of the Tri-Cities Autorama which so far has been viewed by close to 5,000 Tri-Citians.

Doors opened at 4 p.m. Friday and by 6:30, the large hanger in which the many new cars are on display, was packed with thousands of spectators.

Miss Sharon Tate of Richland, a Columbia High School sophomore was named queen of the Autorama before the many applauding spectators Friday night. She is sponsored by Anderson Motors, 941 Stevens, dealers in Chrysler, Plymouth and Studebaker automobiles. Sharon is reigning over the three-day event and tonight will present the grand prize worth several hundred dollars to some lucky spectator.

The grand prize consists of many different items and all will be awarded to one person. These items include: Westinghouse rotisserie; 17-jewel man's wrist watch and expansion band; 9-piece English Sheffield steak and carving set; gear chuck ¼-inch heavy duty electric drill; man's luggage; Proto tool chest; man's leather wallet; 2-piece glass fishing rod; electric pizza baker and broiler oven; Toastwell electric food warmer; Nesco electric sauce pot, giant cooker, fryer; 11-piece treasure chest waterless cookware; chrome pop up toaster; copper and chrome hi-dome electric skillet, copper and chrome automatic electric percolator; giant Duncan Hines outdoor grill with

Autorama Program
SUNDAY
Noon—Opening
3:30.—Style Show
7 p. m.—Style Show
7:30 p. m.—Grand Package Prize awarded
9 p. m.—Closing of 1959 show

roto spit; 3-piece bath mat set; 2-piece salad set; a Fred Leslie Handbag; 4 Marklin miniature autos; 2 3-D viewers; one casserole stand, and a Proto wrench set.

The first annual Autorama is being sponsored by the Tri-City Herald, KALE and Tri-City automobile dealers. Admission is 25 cents for adults and free to children under 12 when accompanied by an adult.

33

Which One Will Be Queen? . . .

NUMBER PLEASE — Judges last night at Desert Inn decided who will be Miss Richland to rule over Atomic Frontier Days, which officially gets under way today. The judges have the number — the number one girl — but candidates above will not know until coronation ceremonies tonight in Riverside Park. Crowning of Miss Richland will be at 8 p.m. Candidates for Miss Richland in the telephone booths awaiting the call from the judges are, left to right, Patti Stewart, Sharon Tate, Patti Crigler, and Dolores Tracy.

(CBNewsphoto)

Sharon Tate Is Atom City Queen

By BILL GASMAN

RICHLAND, Wash., Aug. 6.—Highlighted by the crowning of 16-year-old Sharon Tate as Miss Richland, the 12th annual Atomic Frontier Days celebration got off to a rousing start tonight.

The winner of the coveted honor was announced during the coronation festivities at Riverside park. Miss Tate is the daughter of Capt. and Mrs. Paul Tate and was sponsored by 16th headquarters, Fifth artillery group at Camp Hanford.

The striking beauty intends to be a model after her graduation from high school and has been active in school and community functions.

Candidates

The candidates included Patti Stewart, sponsored by the Richland Veterans of Foreign Wars post; Dolores Tracy, backed by the local unit of National Secretaries association, and Patti Crigler, sponsored by the Loyal Order of Moose.

The community celebration is sponsored by the junior chamber of commerce. Many civic organizations in the area assist in staging the gala affair.

The affair actually started last night when the preliminary judging of the candidates took place. The midway concessions sponsored by various groups in the community will operate each night until the final "go round" on Sunday.

Topping the bill of fare for tomorrow will be the teen night starting at 7:30 p. m. in the park. This will include a talent show, style show, teen dance and other special activities for young and old. A concert by the army band will precede this feature.

to this event and the color and splendor of the fireworks can be viewed for miles around.

Over $4000 has been allocated by the jaycees for the show and celebration this year and nothing has been spared to give the public a good time, according to Fred Fields, general chairman of the function.

SHARON TATE

Sharon being crowned Miss Richland, Washington, August, 1959.

All Eyes on Sharon Tate

1960–1964

Sharon and me with our little sister Patti, Verona, Italy, c. 1960.

"I guess you could say that I was somewhat withdrawn from my classmates. I spent a good deal of time being a loner. I suppose that had something to do with the way we lived—always on the move, never living in one town very long. It's very hard to make lasting friendships that way. And my father was rather strict with me and my two younger sisters. He insisted on proper behavior and very often vetoed our choices of boyfriends. There was always a curfew whenever my sister or I would go out on a date—we had to be home on time or else. But I never resented his authority. In fact, I'm thankful for my strict upbringing; I feel it has helped me learn discipline—and that's very important in this business."

SHARON TATE

TOP AND OPPOSITE Early modeling assignments, Verona, c. 1960

BOTTOM This photograph appeared on the cover of *Stars and Stripes*, 1960.

Bambini Park — Verona, Italy, 1960

As a seven-year-old child, I recall Sharon at the age of seventeen, a blossoming young woman. At the time we were living in Verona, Italy, where my father, an Army Officer, was stationed. Already a lovely flower, my big Sis was the one member of my very strict family who always let me be myself. One time in particular, I vividly remember her allowing me to roller skate across the marble terrace above the two-car garage of our family home. Our horrified housekeeper, Rina, would stick her head out the door and shout in her cute broken English, "Hey Signorina Sharon, you know the Signora does not want her to do that. She may lose control and fall off the balcony." Sharon would reply, "Rina, please let her have some fun. She enjoys it so much. We are not hurting anything and I'm watching her. She won't fall." And so around and around I would go, squealing and giggling with delight. Sis seemed to enjoy it, too.

Sharon was always there for me. The two of us were as thick as thieves. Our mother had many social duties as an officer's wife, including bridge club, formal teas with the wives of visiting dignitaries, and the planning of social dinners with heads of state. Sis would help by taking me on excursions while our housekeeper looked after our little sis, Patti. Our happy outings were sometimes a ruse for Sharon to enjoy the company of a young man—and it will come as no surprise that she had little trouble attracting attention from the opposite sex.

I loved when she took me to Bambini Park, a children's wonderland with slides, swings, monkey bars, and castles to climb and conquer with the other boys and girls. But nothing compared to my personal favorite: the pedal cars. I remember once, overwhelmed by a sense of competition (even at that young age) I eagerly ran and grabbed my car of choice and joined the other children racing around the track. On the first lap, I spotted Sharon nestling herself onto a bench under the shade of a large tree. Next lap, I noticed that a young man had joined her. I lapped again; this time to see the young man had scooted closer. The next lap, his arm was around her. The next, she had slipped his arm off. The next, he leaned in for a kiss. Arghhh, NO! Fortunately, Sharon had turned her head in the nick of time so the kiss landed clumsily on her cheek. Nonetheless, I immediately abandoned my car to run over and save her. You see in my house, Dad had always referred to this particular act of affection as "a monkey bite" and *nobody* was going to *bite* my sister. I approached the two of them ready for battle. She giggled while fending me off the young man.

Truth be told, I think Sharon really appreciated the timing of my entrance, as it got her out of an awkward situation. Having successfully chased off the young admirer, Sis and I strolled off to enjoy an ice cream cone before making our way back home.

TOP AND BOTTOM Sharon is crowned "Queen of the Prom," at Vincenza American High School's homecoming dance, November 1960.

High School graduation photo, Verona, Italy, 1961

"Dear God, she was beautiful. Sharon was more beautiful as a teenager than she was in her twenties; in Europe people would turn around on the street just to look at her."

DORIS TATE (Mother)

OPPOSITE c. 1961 **ABOVE** In 1961 Sharon and her friends answered an ad that appeared in the school newspaper at Vincenza American High School looking for extras for the film *Barabbas*, starring Anthony Quinn and Jack Palance. Sharon appears briefly in the crowd scene as a Patrician.

47

Verona, 1961

"She walked into my office and sat down across from me on the couch. I almost slid off my chair. I mean she was like a blast. And I'm looking at this girl and I'm saying, 'My God, you know, she's really got something.' And I said 'She's not for television, she's for motion picture work.'"

HERB BROWAR (Producer, *The Beverly Hillbillies*)

"Sharon was a lovely young woman. She always seemed a bit cautious when she was on set, as if she was still getting her footing. She was very sweet and seemed eager to learn, though I think she was perhaps a bit intimidated as well. I can't say that she mixed with the rest of the cast. I do remember her laughter though, which rang across the studio."

NANCY KULP (Costar, *The Beverly Hillbillies*)

ABOVE As Janet Trego, *The Beverly Hillbillies*, c. 1964 **OPPOSITE** On set with Max Baer, "The Garden Party" episode of *The Beverly Hillbillies*, August 1, 1963

"My first experience was doing TV commercials. Then one day, my agent sent me to audition for a bit part in *Petticoat Junction*, the TV series. [Producer] Marty (Ransohoff) came on the set, watched me, then called me over and said 'Sweetie, I'm going to make you a star!'"

SHARON TATE

OPPOSITE Sharon (right) with Pat Woodell (as Bobbie Jo), Bea Benaderet (as Kate Bradley), and Linda Kaye Henning (as Betty Jo). *Petticoat Junction*, April 24, 1963. **ABOVE** Sharon (center) with Danica D'Hondt, David McCallum, and Kathy Kersh. "The Girls of Nazarone Affair," episode of *The Man from U.N.C.L.E.*, April 12, 1965.

"In the six years that I knew her, she never said an unkind word about anyone. From the beginning my friends used to tease me, 'How can you wake up in the morning and look at that face of hers?' It was a good question. Sharon was so overwhelmingly, so incredibly beautiful....She had this kind of fragility and you just knew she was bound to get hurt because of it, but you still couldn't help admiring that quality in her. She was such a special person. She was so trusting, so eager to accept people as they were, so generous, she never shut her door to anyone. She always had a way of finding such goodness in others....Sharon was just totally loving and also totally vulnerable. She was a remarkable person—she never gave up on anybody."

SHEILA WELLS (Actress, friend, and roommate)

1965. Photo by Pierluigi Praturlon

"Jay (Sebring) had a private room for his steady clients so that they wouldn't have to be seen by other customers. I had a regular appointment every third week, and it was in that room that I met Sharon Tate. She would often be sitting in a chair, just to be with Jay as he worked. She looked so young that I thought at first she was coming there after school. She wore her blonde hair straight and long. She was quiet and friendly and smiled a lot at our conversations."

DOMINICK DUNNE

ABOVE With boyfriend, celebrated hair stylist Jay Sebring, 1964
OPPOSITE Sharon in a promotional photograph for *Tarzan and the Valley of Gold*, a movie in which she ultimately did not appear.

Cinema segue

SHARON PER FAMIGLIE. Le uniche foto in circolazione prima del debutto newyorchese di Sharon, accreditavano l'immagine di una ragazza bellissima ma non tanto da dispiacere alle casalinghe. Si sapeva che la ragazza aiutava la madre in cucina (sopra), usciva accompagnata dal padre (a sinistra), giocava con le sorelline (a destra), e, come unica distrazione, accettava di fare un giro su veloci auto sportive (sotto).

TRENTA MESI D'INCUBAZIONE. La Filmways, che l'ha scritturata in esclusiva per 7 anni, le ha messo a disposizione una lussuosa villa a Beverly Hills, dove Sharon dai 18 ai 20 anni ha studiato recitazione. Eccola mentre scherza col cane nel giardino.

51

"When Daddy was transferred back to the States and Palos Verdes, California, I convinced him that I'd be safe in Hollywood—you know how Army men are, so terribly protective of their daughters. I've got two sisters, 7 and 13—and Daddy's now in Vietnam, but he still worries about us all."

SHARON TATE

OPPOSITE With Dad, San Pedro, California, c. 1965 **ABOVE** Italian magazine clipping featuring photos of Sharon cooking with Mom, laughing with Dad, and playing tetherball with Patti and me, c. 1965

It was the mid-sixties, I believe. I was flying from Paris where I lived, to Los Angeles to start a film. Could it have been *Cat Ballou*?

I had the window seat and as the plane took off, I turned to the person on my right and found myself sitting next to an extraordinarily beautiful young woman. I was surprised. Usually someone that beautiful is on a private plane. I don't remember ever having a seat-mate that striking. I asked her if she was in the film business and if she was going to L.A. to do a movie. She said she'd done a little work as an extra in Rome but never been in a movie, adding that the producer, Marty Ransohoff, was flying her there to do a screen test for him. We introduced ourselves. She was Sharon Tate. She told me she was living in Italy because her father was in the military. She asked me for any advice I could give her for the upcoming screen test and I remember telling her to just relax and not pretend.

We saw each other from time to time over the years. She came to a party I gave with hair stylist Jay Sebring, and later I went to several parties at the house on Cielo Drive where she and Roman lived. She was very pregnant the last time I saw her at that house and turned down a joint that was being passed around.

She was a sweet woman.

JANE FONDA

Photo by Hatami, c. 1965

"They said they had a plan for me. They would train me and prepare me. I was immediately put into training, like a race horse. I had a job to stay the way I was. They told me 'Cream your face, Sharon.... Put on more eyeliner, Sharon.... Stick out your boobs, Sharon."

SHARON TATE

OPPOSITE AND RIGHT London, 1965

Photo by Hatami, 1965

The
MGM
Years

1965–1967

Making Waves, 1966

In late 1965 Sharon flew to London to begin filming *Eye of the Devil* with David Niven and Kim Novak. In so many ways this was the defining moment she had long anticipated. Sharon's agent, Hal Gefsky, and producer Martin Ransohoff felt strongly that her talents belonged in motion pictures, so they had previously kept her "under wraps" in small roles on television shows like *Mister Ed*, *Petticoat Junction*, and *The Man from U.N.C.L.E.* For an episode of *The Beverly Hillbillies* they even disguised her in a dark wig. The idea was to discreetly allow Sharon to gain experience in front of a camera and sharpen her acting chops before taking her place on the big screen.

Our family was disappointed that we couldn't join Sharon on set in England or on location at the Château de Hautefort in France, but we were kept abreast of events through regular letters and phone calls. It would be an understatement to say that Sharon was intimidated to be working with an acting legend like David Niven, but he was absolutely wonderful to her and that put her at ease. Kim Novak was also very supportive, but she eventually had to be replaced by Deborah Kerr after being seriously injured in a horse-riding accident. At the time the tabloid press unfairly suggested that Ms. Novak had used the accident as an excuse to leave the production because she was jealous of Sharon's youth and beauty. This was completely untrue.

That's not to say Sharon hadn't previously incited envy from a legendary leading lady, as Elizabeth Taylor had reportedly requested she be removed from the set of *The Sandpiper* in 1964. Never recalling Sharon mentioning this at the time, I had the opportunity to ask Ms. Taylor about the incident many years later, when I was working as a makeup artist. In her famous candied voice, she rolled her eyes and deadpanned, "*Of course* I had her removed. Did you ever *see* your sister?" I loved that answer, so I just laughed and continued with my work.

When *Eye of the Devil* was released in America we excitedly rushed to the nearest cinema to see it. Sharon came with us. Sitting in the dark, watching her up there on the big screen, I was mesmerized by her presence. Her talent, her beauty, her sheer "star quality" were absolutely unmistakable. I'm not just saying this because she's my sister, but as the mysterious Odile de Caray Sharon almost literally jumps off the screen—you can't take your eyes off her. Critics and the public seemed to think likewise. To this day, *Eye of the Devil* remains my favorite of Sharon's films.

Her next movie for MGM was much more geographically desirable because it kept Sharon close to our family. Mom, Patti, and I were invited to visit the set of *Don't Make Waves*, and on that day the location was a stretch of beach in Malibu. I was naturally athletic;

however, I must have had more confidence in my physical abilities than I had a right to because I suddenly decided that I was going to take up surfing during our day in Malibu. The night before our visit to the set I borrowed a longboard from one of my guy friends. It was the size of a small boat—the kind of board Frankie and Annette would hang ten on in their movies. The next morning, Patti and I shoved the board into the car as best we could. It went diagonally from the front dash passenger's side and out the back window on the driver's side. Patti and I both sat in the back seat to keep it from becoming airborne, and off we went.

After arriving in Malibu, the surfboard came out of the car with much more difficulty than it went in. After working up a sweat to extract the thing, I proceeded to drag it down to the water's edge. Along the way, a second unit director spotted the board and yelled, "It's perfect!" I looked around to see what he could possibly be referring to—"it" certainly wasn't me. No, *it* was my surfboard. He ran over and tried to remove it from my grip. I don't think he knew I wasn't part of the crew. Then he went over to Sharon as her hair was being worked on and asked, "Excuse me, Miss Tate. Can we just have you pose for a moment in front of this surfboard? The result was a soon-to-be-famous shot of Sharon leaning against my borrowed longboard. It appeared in magazines around the world and was even used in some versions of the foreign language poster art. Tony Curtis and bodybuilder Dave Draper, just off camera preparing for a scene, watched her being photographed with great amusement. I heard Mr. Curtis repeatedly proclaim words to the effect of, "Wow, she sure is stunning," to which Mr. Draper would reply, "She certainly is." Following the impromptu shoot I got my longboard back. I can't exactly say I conquered surfing that day, but I certainly had fun trying.

A few days later we received a very distressing phone call from Sharon. She was more upset than I had ever heard her and the tale she told us was horrifying. She had almost drowned in a scene where she was to jump out of an airplane and into a swimming pool. Her harness malfunctioned. It opened too quickly and that caused the parachute to cover the entire surface of the pool. Sharon was unable to surface for air. Much worse was the fact that the following day, a stuntman on the film lost his life in a similar accident. After landing in the Pacific Ocean, his parachute kept him from surfacing and help came too late. I will never forget the deep sorrow this accident caused the entire cast and crew for the duration of the film.

Sharon with Patti
and me, c. 1965

Metro-Goldwyn-Mayer présente
DEBORAH KERR · DAVID NIVEN
DONALD PLEASENCE
dans une production
MARTIN RANSOHOFF
LE MYSTÈRE DES TREIZE
EYE OF THE DEVIL
EDWARD MULHARE · FLORA ROBSON · EMLYN WILLIAMS & SHARON TATE
REALISATION J. LEE THOMPSON · PRODUCTION JOHN CALLEY & MARTIN RANSOHOFF · FILMWAYS PICTURE ·
MGM
HET OOG VAN DE DUIVEL

"Sharon was asked to play this very difficult role, of a rather witchlike person. It was asking a newcomer to do a lot. She takes direction beautifully. Very soon she began to realize that the camera was a friend. 'Could she do it?' that was in all our minds. We even agreed that if after the first two weeks, Sharon was not quite making it, that we would put her back in cold storage. We started work. The moment that Sharon appeared on screen in her first rushes, we knew that this wonderful personality was going to make out. We all realized that here was a girl who was tremendously exciting. She had that thing that you can't really explain, Star projection. I think this girl is going to be a big big star."

J. LEE THOMPSON (Director, *Eye of the Devil*, 1966)

Sharon as Odile de Caray, *Eye of the Devil*, 1966

Eye of the Devil, 1966

"Sharon is a great discovery. First of all, she's a fabulously good looking bird and she's got all the fun and spark and go. She's a marvelous girl. She's up on cloud nine, Sharon is. And I think she's a very, very good actress. She's obviously going to make a big hit in this picture."

DAVID NIVEN (Costar, *Eye of the Devil*, 1966)

On set with David Niven. *Eye of the Devil*, 1966

"I'd like to be an American Catherine Deneuve. She plays beautiful, sensitive, deep parts with a little bit of intelligence behind them."

SHARON TATE

ABOVE (LEFT) On set with director J. Lee Thompson, *Eye of the Devil*
ABOVE (RIGHT) With David Niven (as Philippe de Montfaucon)
OPPOSITE *Eye of the Devil*

Sharon Tate's intent is evil as she shows her Eye of the Devil necklace to the children who react with hypnotic fascination.

MGM presents "EYE OF THE DEVIL" A MARTIN RANSOHOFF PRODUCTION

David Niven holds high court over the bizarre hooded members of the secret "13" cult as Sharon Tate kneels before him during the ceremony.

MGM presents "EYE OF THE DEVIL" A MARTIN RANSOHOFF PRODUCTION

Devil worshiper Sharon Tate offers a white dove, killed in flight by an archer's arrow, as sacrifice to the demands of the unholy "13" tribunal.

MGM presents "EYE OF THE DEVIL" A MARTIN RANSOHOFF PRODUCTION

"Sharon had a fragile, incandescent quality that brought oxygen into the room."

YUL BRYNNER

On the set of *Eye of the Devil*, 1966. Photo by Gérard Decaux

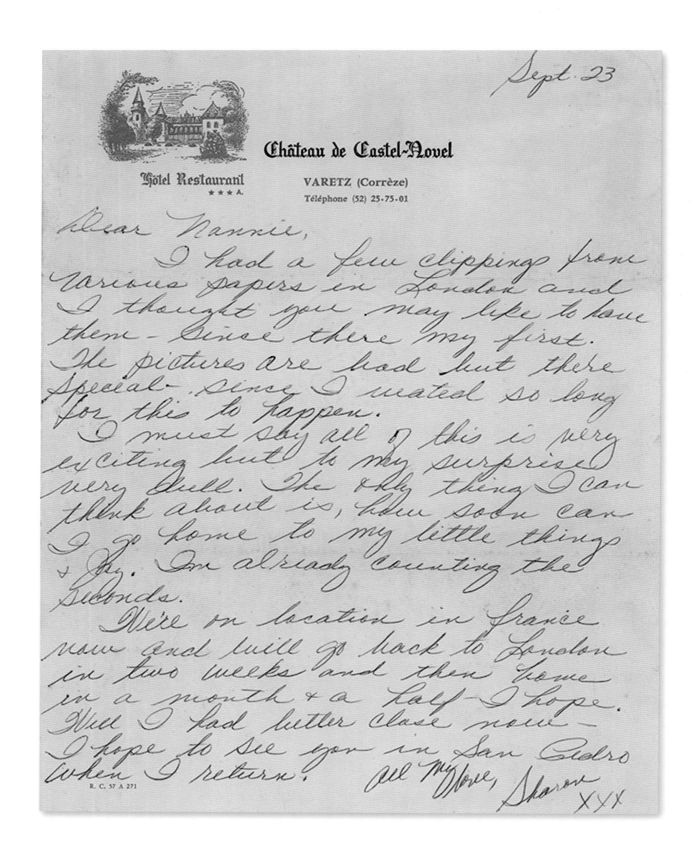

Sept. 23

Château de Castel-Novel

Hôtel Restaurant
★★★ A.

VARETZ (Corrèze)
Téléphone (52) 25-75-01

Dear Nannie,

I had a few clippings from various papers in London and I thought you may like to have them — since there my first. The pictures are bad but there special. Since I waited so long for this to happen.

I must say all of this is very exciting but to my surprise very dull. The only thing I can think about is, how soon can I go home to my little things & Jay. I'm already counting the seconds.

We're on location in France now and will go back to London in two weeks and then home in a month & a half — I hope. Well I had better close now — I hope to see you in San Pedro when I return!

All my love,
Sharon
xxx

R. C. 57 A 271

ABOVE A letter home to Nannie Tate **OPPOSITE** Sharon at home in London, during the filming of *Eye of the Devil*. Photo by Araldo di Crollalanza

"I liked her very much, you know. I'd always admired her as a little girl, and when I grew up and finally met her I wasn't disappointed. She was everything I'd ever imagined her to be. And she was marvelous to me— so thoughtful, so kind, so helpful."

SHARON TATE (on Kim Novak who had to drop out of *Eye of the Devil* and be replaced by Deborah Kerr)

OPPOSITE September 27, 1965. Photo by Philippe Le Tellier   **ABOVE (LEFT)** Magazine article
ABOVE (RIGHT) With Kim Novak (as Catherine de Montfaucon), *Eye of the Devil*, 1966

"Sharon had real talent. She was going to be a big star."

DEBORAH KERR

ABOVE With Deborah Kerr (as Catherine de Montfaucon), *Eye of the Devil*
OPPOSITE On set with director J. Lee Thompson and Deborah Kerr

"I'm very unpredictable. Very, very impulsive. Extremely. Absolutely! Sometimes I don't know what I want to do from one day to the next. I can't enjoy anything premeditated; I just do it as I feel it. But whatever I do is motivated by honesty."

SHARON TATE

On location at the Château de Hautefort, France, *Eye of the Devil*, September 27, 1965. Photo by Philippe Le Tellier

"Beauty is only a look. It has nothing to do with what I'm like inside."

SHARON TATE

"I first saw her on the Santa Monica pier, and all I could think of was: 'This is the sexiest girl I ever saw in my life.' She was wearing Italian sandals and tight blue jeans and a navy-blue T-shirt that made the most of her midriff; her hair was tied up in a man's silk print handkerchief and she wore absolutely no makeup, but nobody on the beach could see anything but her. It's almost embarrassing."

REX REED

"An exceptional body and an amazing face, stunning!"

TONY CURTIS

ABOVE AND OPPOSITE Tony Curtis (as Carlo Cofield) and Sharon (as Malibu), *Don't Make Waves*, 1967

"I will never be another Marilyn Monroe, but I had to do what they wanted at first. They see me as a dolly in a bikini, jumping up and down on a trampoline."

SHARON TATE

OPPOSITE With Dave Draper (as Harry Hollard), *Don't Make Waves*, 1967 **ABOVE** I took this photograph of Sharon with Tony Curtis between takes during the filming of *Don't Make Waves*, 1967.

103

I think of Sharon often as pictures of her during our filming of *Don't Make Waves* adorn the walls of my gym in Santa Cruz, California. The members are mesmerized. She's a star in the eyes of my heart not only because of her physical and internal beauty but also for her earthy courage and daring spontaneity. Sharon was a year younger than I, and several solid steps ahead, when we met on the set of a film called *Don't Make Waves*, in which we costarred. It was nearly half a century ago but seems like yesterday. We became friends like kids in school, I being the guy who carried her books. She was wrapped up with Roman Polanski and I was married. She felt unthreatened, and we could pal around and travel together when promotions required our presence. She held onto my arm and wouldn't let go as our four-passenger aircraft worked its way through a storm on a flight to Charlotte for a film promotion, yet she didn't hesitate to leap high from a trampoline and into my arms again and again to complete a beach scene in the making. We hung in the shade and talked about this or that or nothing with the rest of the crew till it was our turn to tumble in the forsaken house in Malibu.

Sharon, Miss Tate, was gutsy, energetic, athletic, willing and able, and absolutely beautiful. She was honest and innocent. Two years after our film experience, as I walked across the LAX terminal, an enthusiastic voice called "Dave, Dave, Dave" across the deserted late-night floor. I turned and it was Sharon dressed in black and wearing high-heeled boots. She ran and jumped into my arms, excitedly introduced me to her young friends, and was off. That was the last I saw of the beautiful girl. Not many people got to know Sharon Tate very well. The dear child, the beautiful woman, lived only twenty-six years. I met her during one of those precious years when life was brimming with promise and flooded with sunshine. We passed in the night like lost friends. I miss her today.

DAVE DRAPER (Costar, *Don't Make Waves*, 1967)

With Dave Draper, *Don't Make Waves*, 1967

Join the tan-ables . . . get the best of the sun

Sharon Tate
Co-starring in Martin Ransohoff's
"Don't Make Waves" says —

"Coppertone gives you a *better* tan"

(—it's enriched to give extra protection, too!)

You *do* get a better tan with Coppertone. The fastest tan possible with maximum sunburn protection . . . plus extra safe-guards against skin dryness. Coppertone contains the most widely beach-tested sunscreen. It's also enriched with lanolin, cocoa butter and other moisturizers that make your skin more tan-able . . . keep your skin soft and satiny sleek.

So join the tan-ables. Get a better tan . . . deep, dark, superbly smooth. Coppertone outsells them all because it out-tans them all! Get the best of the sun with enriched Coppertone. Save on large size.

TAN, DON'T BURN—with America's most popular, most complete *line* of suntan products: *Lotion, Oil, Cream, Spray, Shade®, Noskote®, Lipkote®, Royal Blend®. Also new Baby Tan® for young children and Royal Blend Soap.*

17

ABOVE Coppertone promotional advertisment for *Don't Make Waves*, 1967 **RIGHT** Sharon on the *Don't Make Waves* set, using my surfboard as a prop between takes.

"Sharon Tate was such an amazing person, worldly, but not in any negative ways. She was so grounded, still seemed to show such delight in the little things. A good waiter or waitress in a restaurant, a terrific sunset, ANY animal, little tiny things never lost their magic for her. She had the world at her feet, but never lost touch with who she was, or became blasé about how fortunate she had become. The superficiality of the movie world didn't fool her one bit, she often said, 'If I start to believe I'm as good as they keep telling me I am, I'll get out, there's still so much to learn.'"

CLAUDIA CARDINALE (Costar, *Don't Make Waves*, 1967)

ABOVE With Tony Curtis, *Don't Make Waves*, 1967
RIGHT Following her near-drowning accident on the
set of *Don't Make Waves*, 1967

"I'm so afraid of hurting other people's feelings. I don't speak out when I should. I get into big messes that way."

SHARON TATE

As Sarah Shagal in *The Fearless Vampire Killers*, 1967. Photo by Roman Polanski

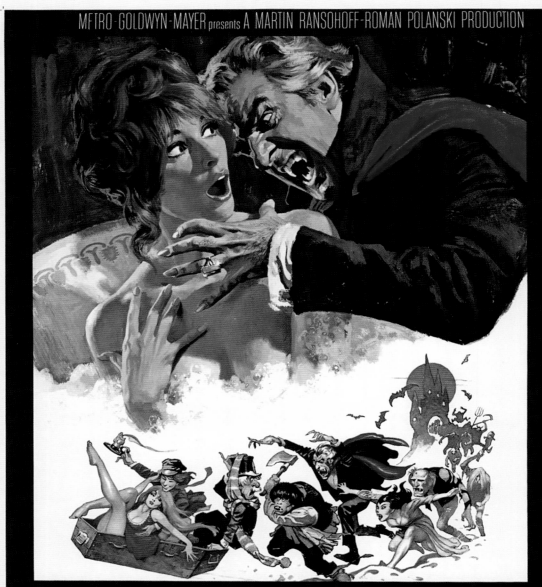

"Martin Ransohoff had to sell Roman on the idea of even considering me for the film. He arranged for the two of us to have dinner. Roman never said a word to me, we just sat there and ate and he just looked at me. Then we had a second dinner meeting and the same thing happened. Later he took me to his apartment. He lit some candles and then excused himself and left me standing there alone. A short while later he came storming into the room like a madman and he was wearing a Frankenstein mask. I let out a bloodcurdling scream and while I was still crying from the scare, he was calling Ransohoff to tell him that the part in the film was mine."

SHARON TATE (on how she received the part of Sarah Shagal in Roman Polanski's *The Fearless Vampire Killers*, 1967)

159-3

159-7

159-4

159-8

159-5

159-9

ABOVE Being directed by Roman during the filming of *The Fearless Vampire Killers*, 1967 **OPPOSITE** With Roman (as Alfred) in *The Fearless Vampire Killers*

This is the year Sharon Tate happens. A screen newcomer with three films to be released in 1967, Sharon shows best in Roman Polanski's *The Vampire Killers*, a slap-stick unreeling of macabre carryings-on. Says director Polanski, who last year shocked movie-goers with *Repulsion*, "What kind of film is *The Vampire Killers*? It's funny!" A man of many talents, Polanski, who co-stars in his new movie, personally photographed Sharon for the pages of PLAYBOY. Depicted here is her sudsy tête-à-Tate with a frightening film ghoul who, like us, finds Sharon a tasty dish, indeed.

The Tate Gallery:

PICTURES BY POLANSKI

"The Vampire Killers" displays Sharon's formidable form in two tub-thumping scenes. Signed by Martin Ransohoff to a Filmways contract four years ago, she received a half-million-dollar Hollywood non-buildup: continuous courses in everything from diction to dancing to dress— even bodybuilding. Says Miss Tate, "Mr. Ransohoff didn't want the audience to see me till I was ready." As Polanski's photos reveal, Sharon's ready now.

Cast as an innkeeper's daughter, Sharon proves too tempting a bathing beauty for vampire Count Krolock (Ferdy Mayne) to bypass. The no'-count villain quickly turns Sharon into a fellow vamp, and together, the gruesome twosome terrorize the citizenry of—where else?— Transylvania.

OPPOSITE *The Fearless Vampire Killers*, 1967
ABOVE *Playboy* magazine featuring "Pictures by Polanski," 1967

METRO-GOLDWYN-MAYER présente

LE BAL DES VAMPIRES

INTERDIT AUX MOINS DE 13 ANS

avec JACK MacGOWRAN · SHARON TATE · ALFIE BASS
et avec FERDY MAYNE

Scénario de ROMAN POLANSKI et GERARD BRACH · Réalisation de ROMAN POLANSKI · Production de GENE GUTOWSKI
Une production CADRE FILMS · FILMWAYS **PANAVISION-METROCOLOR**

Visa n° 2672

"Sharon Tate was so beautiful. Roman Polanski, he was the man. He saw me in a television interview and liked the look of me. He cast me as a bloody monster, a hunchback with a deformed face and a club foot…I spent three months in the snow. I enjoyed it. Sharon was snowboarding, or whatever, for six weeks."

TERRY DOWNES (Costar, *The Fearless Vampire Killers*, 1967)

ABOVE With Terry Downes (as Koukol, the Servant), *The Fearless Vampire Killers* **OPPOSITE** *The Fearless Vampire Killers*

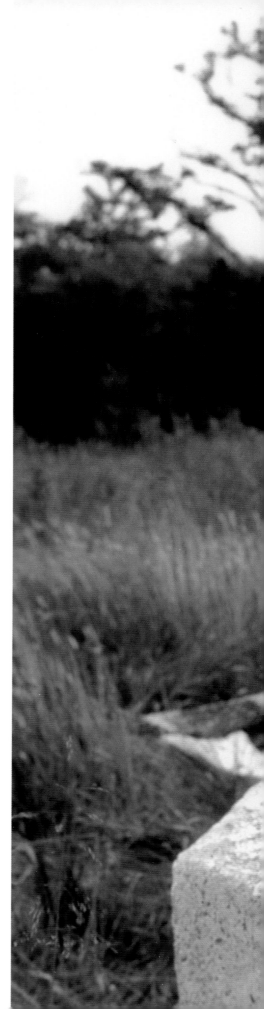

ABOVE AND RIGHT On the set of *The Fearless Vampire Killers*, 1967

Valley
of the
Dolls

1967

Left to Right: Barbara Parkins (as Anne Welles), Sharon (as Jennifer North), and Patty Duke (as Neely O'Hara). *Valley of the Dolls*, 1967

"*Valley of the Dolls*, that candy box of vulgarity with something for everyone has, at last, reached its big-money mecca. Jacqueline Susann's super-selling book is now, what else? A motion picture, shot in, where else? Hollywood, the place that understands it best. . . . [*Dolls*] is a gargantuan saga of three girls and the nasty, cheesy, show-bizzy world they live in, which drives them not only to drink but to 'dolls,' which are pills other than aspirin. . . . Sporting $1,300 worth of false hair, *Dolls* stars Barbara Parkins (left), Sharon Tate and Patty Duke loll on the film's most persuasive piece of furniture."

Look magazine (September 5, 1967)

Valley of the Dolls

Following her success at MGM, Sharon hit the ground running in 1967 with a new contract at mega-studio 20th Century Fox. In a casting fiasco that recalled the search for Scarlett O'Hara in *Gone With the Wind*, Sis was quickly awarded the choice role of Jennifer North in *Valley of the Dolls*. Fox wasted no time in snapping up the rights to Jacqueline Susann's controversial 1966 blockbuster about Hollywood life in the fast lane. Every top actress, from Raquel Welch to Candice Bergen auditioned for the role, but Fox, forever looking to replace the unfortunate loss of Marilyn Monroe five years earlier, sought to capitalize on Sharon's extreme beauty and set the publicity machine spinning in its promotion of their new star.

As none of the family had been able to see Sharon on the set of *The Fearless Vampire Killers* the previous year, she arranged for us to watch a day of filming on *Valley of the Dolls*. We were all very excited. I was on spring break, so I decided to fly down early from Sausalito and relax for a few days with Sis at her house on the Pacific Coast Highway. It was right on the sand next to the Santa Monica Pier, and I spent my mornings body surfing in front of the house and helped Sharon run lines after lunch.

I remember working on the scene where she is on the phone

with her needy and overcritical mother. I took the role of the mother. We ran the scene over and over, working on the timing of the pauses between lines, the inflection of her voice, and her facial expressions. Later, when she actually shot the scene there was no one on the other end of the line, which of course made it very difficult, as there was no interaction between characters. The scene was very poignant and extremely important to Sharon, as it established her character's motivation for the rest of the film.

By late afternoon we usually walked over to the pier and paused for a few moments to view the spectacular colors of the sky and setting sun, before embarking on a mission of devouring a hot dog and soda or whatever form of junk food that struck our fancy. It was such a wonderful time in life. All I could think was, "It doesn't get any better than this." Meanwhile, back in Sausalito, Mom and Patti packed up the car and prepared to head south to L.A. just as soon as Dad could shake free of his duties. They also brought a surprise for Sis with them—a Yorkie puppy that Sharon named Sapirstein, after the doctor's character in Roman's film *Rosemary's Baby*. We all met up at the great 20th Century Fox studios. This would be the first time any of us got to see Sharon work on a sound stage.

The morning we arrived at the studio, Sharon was already in hair and makeup. I stuck close to Sis and kept her company while she was being prepared for camera. A self-proclaimed athlete and tomboy, I was surprisingly enthralled at the glamorous spectacle of assistants, makeup artists, hairstylists, and designers buzzing around the dressing rooms. Sharon sat patiently and studied her face in the mirror as Ben Nye, the head of Fox's makeup department, applied a slightly warm foundation that perfectly matched her honeyed, yet extremely pale, natural skin tone. Nye's makeup design for Sharon took its cue from the world of high fashion and adapted to the times by shifting focus from the bold and brazen lips of the fifties to the theatrically embellished eyes of the sixties. Resurrecting a technique used by Greta Garbo in the 1930s, Nye accentuated Sharon's enormous eyes with a half-moon (or "banana" as it was referred to back then) of natural eyeliner in the crease of the lid that deepened the socket and gave her face the appearance of a beautiful doe. After lining each outer corner underneath the eye, lower individual false eyelashes were applied and coated with clear mascara, while a single or double row of feathered or spiked false eyelashes were applied to the top lids to complete the look. She also sported newly refined eyebrows that were brushed upward and glued into place to complement the lines of the false eyelashes. Lips were toned down in soft hues of nude or pink with a creamy (and never glossy) finish, to keep attention focused on the eyes.

Sharon's hairstylist was a small lady named Kay Pownall, who worked under the direction of Kenneth Battelle (or just "Kenneth," as he was professionally known). Kenneth was credited in the film as designing exclusively for Barbara Parkins, but he actually created hairstyles for all the leads. Kay applied multiple hairpieces to Sharon's head after teasing her hair to the point of torture, but the finished result was, of course, worth it. The coiffures in *Valley of the Dolls* were strongly influenced by current trends and the flamboyant ebullience of Diana Vreeland, then editor-in-chief of American *Vogue*. Such explosions of fantasy—especially the ones worn by Sharon in the nightclub scene and Barbara Parkins in the "Gillian Girl" commercial—were sometimes made architecturally possible by assembling swatches or braids of swirling Dynel to a solid infrastructure. These dramatic, seemingly impossible hairstyles, often paired with the kind of exaggerated makeup usually revered by drag queens, electrified the pages of *Bazaar* and *Vogue*, which at the time dubbed it "The Beauty Look." *Valley of the Dolls* rode the wave of this "mod" trend and the film's high camp look has today greatly contributed to its longevity and enormous popularity.

Fox also ensured the movie would hit a glamorous high note by placing legendary designer William Travilla at the fashion helm. Most famous for Marilyn Monroe's "skirt blowing" dress in *The Seven Year Itch*, Travilla created a series of mostly halter dresses and sequined gowns for Sharon, constructed to discreetly reveal the body while giving the illusion of height. My personal favorites were the white gown from the nightclub sequence and the striped lamé shift dress with matching coat from the scene where her screen husband, Tony Polar, falls down the stairs.

The lily gilded and glamorized, Sharon was ready for her close-up. Then began the usual waiting game as director Mark Robson and the lighting men adjusted the stage. Sharon introduced us to Barbara Parkins and Patty Duke, who were very gracious and made us all feel at home. Lee Grant, perhaps adhering to some method technique and her character's stern demeanor, was very nice but kept mostly to herself. Sis was quite nervous to be playing opposite an actress of Ms. Grant's accomplishments. She seemed to sense this and was noticeably patient with Sharon.

Although we were welcome family members, there is always the feeling when being on set that you are somewhat in the way. With this in mind, I noticed Dad become increasingly uncomfortable. Perhaps feeling he had no business being around dressing rooms and the like, he decided to wander off and take in some of the other sights that the 20th Century Fox backlot had to offer. Later he returned and enthusiastically announced that he had been invited to the set of Fox's other major film in production—*Planet of the Apes*. I was beside myself. Watching my sister tear up the scenery with dueling divas in wigs was one thing, but the opportunity to see Cornelius and Zira was more than I could resist. Dad and I discretely exited, leaving

Mom and Patti to observe Sharon and Lee Grant in a scene.

Looking back at this moment, my father was responsible for bringing me to what would become my career as a makeup artist many years later. The wonders taking place on the *Apes* set were mesmerizing. To me, it was an art form—a whole new level of creativity that I just knew I had to be a part of. Dad saw that I had caught the bug as I was the only other artist in the family and he always encouraged me in my career choice. To this day, I firmly believe that my brief experiences on the sets of *Dolls* and *Planet of the Apes*, engrossed in the processes of fantasy and reinvention, significantly changed the course of my life.

Valley of the Dolls premiered in December of that year and despite mixed reviews was an immediate box-office blockbuster. Sharon was nominated the following February for a Golden Globe Award as 1967's "Most Promising Female Newcomer." Time has since deified the film and today it is considered a camp classic with an enormous following that continues to grow. It was many decades before I had the opportunity to watch *Dolls* again, but what struck me was Sharon's wonderful performance. She is touching as Jennifer North, and the only understated character in a film certainly not known for restraint.

In the Valley of the Dolls, it's instant turn-on...dolls to put you to sleep at night, kick you awake in the morning, make life seem great—instant love, instant excitement... ultimate hell!

Valley of the Dolls

THE MOTION PICTURE THAT SHOWS WHAT AMERICA'S ALL TIME #1 BEST SELLER FIRST PUT INTO WORDS!

20th CENTURY-FOX Presents
A MARK ROBSON · DAVID WEISBART PRODUCTION

Starring
BARBARA PARKINS · PATTY DUKE · PAUL BURKE · SHARON TATE · TONY SCOTTI · LEE GRANT

GUEST STARS
JOEY BISHOP · GEORGE JESSEL

SUSAN HAYWARD as Helen Lawson

SUGGESTED FOR MATURE AUDIENCES

Produced by DAVID WEISBART   Directed by MARK ROBSON   Screenplay by HELEN DEUTSCH and DOROTHY KINGSLEY   Songs by DORY and ANDRE PREVIN
Based on a Book by JACQUELINE SUSANN   DIONNE WARWICK sings "Valley of the Dolls" theme   PANAVISION® COLOR by DeLUXE   ORIGINAL SOUND TRACK ALBUM AVAILABLE ON 20th CENTURY-FOX RECORDS

The Producers wish to state that any similarity between any person, living or dead, and the characters portrayed in this film is purely coincidental and not intended.

67/275

"She had the most exquisite face I have ever seen. She was gentle and she was kind. And there wasn't a mean bone in that girl's body....I remember the impact she had on anyone watching her when we filmed our scenes in *Valley*. She was mesmerizing and held everyone's attention, even when she was not the main focus."

BARBARA PARKINS (Costar, *Valley of the Dolls*, 1967)

As Jennifer North, *Valley of the Dolls*, 1967. Photo by Curt Gunther

"I got to know Sharon during our time together filming *Valley of the Dolls*. We spent a lot of time talking, mostly about Roman, and going to the movies. She was a wonderful person."

TONY SCOTTI
(Costar, *Valley of the Dolls*, 1967)

With Tony Scotti (as Tony Polar), *Valley of the Dolls*, 1967

"Being in Sharon's presence, was being enveloped in grace. Her inner beauty superseded her outer beauty, if you can imagine. Once in a while she'd catch me staring at her in awe."

PATTY DUKE (Costar, *Valley of the Dolls*, 1967)

Valley of the Dolls, 1967. Photos by Louis Goldman

TOP Original costume sketches by Travilla for Sharon's character, Jennifer North
BOTTOM LEFT With William Travilla. **BOTTOM RIGHT** With William Travilla and Barbara Parkins

"Sharon Tate is divine, a real find. Just wait and see what happens when the critics and public see her in *Valley of the Dolls*. Sharon has everything Marilyn Monroe had—and more. She has the fascinating, yet wholly feminine strength of a Dietrich or a Garbo…a classically beautiful face, an exciting figure, the kind of sex appeal and personality appeal to become as glittering a star as Bette Davis, Joan Crawford, Rita Hayworth, Lana Turner, or Elizabeth Taylor."

TRAVILLA (Costume designer, *Valley of the Dolls*, 1967)

LADIES
WARDROBE
PICTURE A-871   Date 5/8/67
TITLE VALLEY OF THE DOLLS
DIRECTOR MARK ROBSON
ACTRESS SHARON TATE
PART JENNIFER NORTH
CHANGE No. 8
INT + EXT. MUSIC CENTER
INT + EXT BEDROOM
SCENE No. 151-153 TO 157
TRAVILLA   8 x 10

Valley of the Dolls, 1967

"I am like Jennifer (Sharon's character in *Valley of the Dolls*) because she is relatively simple, a victim of circumstances beyond her control. But I have more confidence in myself."

SHARON TATE

With Lee Grant (as Miriam Polar), *Valley of the Dolls*, 1967

"You know it's funny, I fondly remember how Sharon was always sneaking a cigarette. Roman didn't like her smoking, such a silly little thing to remember, but it always makes me smile. We would always laugh about it."

LEE GRANT (Costar, *Valley of the Dolls*, 1967)

"Sharon has this amazing quality, an enormous screen presence, you can't take your eyes off her. She's a very vulnerable girl, but turns that into some terrific acting."

MARK ROBSON (Director, *Valley of the Dolls*, 1967)

ABOVE On set with director Mark Robson, *Valley of the Dolls*, 1967

"Sharon Tate emerges as the film's most sympathetic character, who takes an overdose of sleeping pills when breast cancer threatens to rob her of her only means of livelihood. William Daniels' photographic caress of her faultless face and enormous absorbent eyes is stunning."

THE HOLLYWOOD REPORTER

"I read that I'm supposed to be Hollywood's new sex symbol, that Marty has groomed me as Marilyn Monroe's replacement. I think I'm the most unsexy thing that ever was. I'm open for everything of course, but I'm certainly not aware of being sexy."

SHARON TATE

queen

16 February   Fortnightly 3s 6d

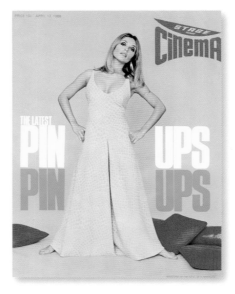

158

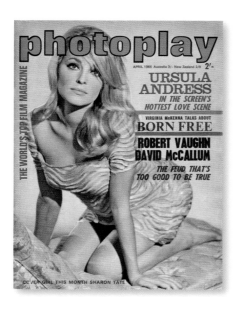

photoplay

THE WORLD'S TOP FILM MAGAZINE

APRIL 1966 Australia 3/- New Zealand 2/9   2/-

URSULA ANDRESS
IN THE SCREEN'S HOTTEST LOVE SCENE

VIRGINIA McKENNA TALKS ABOUT
BORN FREE

ROBERT VAUGHN DAVID McCALLUM
THE FEUD THAT'S TOO GOOD TO BE TRUE

COVER GIRL THIS MONTH SHARON TATE

KINEJUN *show times*

キネマ旬報   下旬号   **8**

■増刊号■吉田喜重の言葉■座談
会と研究「私はジプシー
の唄をきいた」論■「私が棄
てた女」論■「別離」特
集■シナリオ「いのち」
ぼうにふろう物語」陸巴

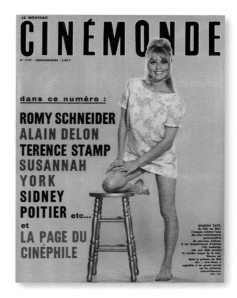

LE NOUVEAU

CINÉMONDE

N° 1757 - HEBDOMADAIRE - 2,50 7

dans ce numéro :

ROMY SCHNEIDER
ALAIN DELON
TERENCE STAMP
SUSANNAH YORK
SIDNEY POITIER etc...
et
LA PAGE DU CINÉPHILE

SHARON TATE, de fille en fille...

O CRUZEIRO

EM CÔRES
O FILME DOS
BEATLES

EXCLUSIVO
A VITÓRIA
DO BRASIL
NO GAÚCHÃO

VOCÊ É
ALCOÓLATRA?

BEIRA-RIO
O MARACANÃ DE
PORTO ALEGRE

SÃO PAULO
A VOLTA DE
ÉDER JOFRE

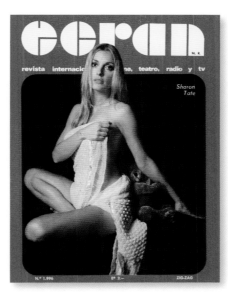

eran

revista internacional de cine, teatro, radio y tv

Sharon Tate

N.° 1.996   B° 2.-   ZIG-ZAG

wm
WOMEN'S MIRROR

WITCHES '66:
that old black magic
turns white

HOW FAR FROM FAME?
SIX FACES GOING PLACES
This one belongs to Sharon Tate

Parade
Oakland Tribune

IS THE GOVERNMENT
WATCHING YOU
TOO CLOSELY?
By JACK ANDERSON

SHARON TATE:
"Sweetie, I'm going
to make you a star!"
by LLOYD SHEARER

September 18,

NUEVO
FOTOGRAMAS

La última
película de
SHARON
TATE

Las confesiones de
JOSÉ LUIS
LÓPEZ VÁZQUEZ

triunfo

AÑO XXI - NÚM. 319 - 9 DE JULIO DE 1969 - 15 PESETAS

SHARON TATE

HACE 25 AÑOS
OPERACIÓN
BARBARROJA
*
CINE JOVEN:
MAYORÍA DE EDAD
'LA CAZA'

Portfolio

1964–1969

The Eye of the Beholder

---○---

Sharon's love affair with the camera began at an early age. She adored being photographed. While all babies are beautiful, at six months she resembled a Raphael cherub and was crowned "Miss Tiny Tot" of Dallas. As she grew into a teenager, and her more unique physical qualities became apparent, Sharon enjoyed considerable success on the local pageant circuit. Though certainly confident about her looks, she never flaunted them, and actually downplayed her attractiveness during her teenage years.

I always saw Sharon's face as a constantly evolving work of art. She was, of course, extraordinarily photogenic. That term suggests a magic that occurs between subject and lens as light is reflected off the planes of the face and is then captured on film. For this reason, what we sometimes see of a face in person, in three dimensions, can differ considerably from what the camera presents as reality.

It is generally agreed that the photogenic face combines symmetry; large, wide-set eyes; defined bone structure; and a smaller nose with minimal projection (to avoid overly conspicuous shadows). Sharon was the genetic blueprint of this formula.

In late October of 1966, Sharon flew to New York to be photographed by the great Richard Avedon for a magazine photo-say titled "The World's Most Beautiful Women." It was a huge achievement for Sharon and a solid validation that she had finally arrived. At the height of his powers, Avedon's dramatic portraits movie stars, rock stars, presidents, and royalty captivated a generation, while his highly original style of fashion photography—featuring iconic models like Jean Shrimpton, Veruschka, Penelope Tree, and Twiggy—dominated the pages of magazines around the world and significantly defined the look of what we fondly refer to as the "Swinging Sixties."

As time progressed, and her celebrity grew, Sharon would go on to work with some of the most important photographers of the twentieth century, including Bert Stern, Philippe Halsman, David Bailey, Milton Greene, Norman Parkinson, John Engstead, Neal Barr, Terry O'Neill, Jerry Schatzberg, David McCabe, and Pierluigi Praturlon. Both *Vogue* and *Harper's Bazaar* featured her as a celebrity model.

One photographer she shared a very special artist/muse relationship with was Shahrokh Hatami. Professionally known as "Hatami," he started his career as a writer for a major newspaper in Tehran before switching to photojournalism. His candid portraits of Elizabeth Taylor, Marlon Brando, Sophia Loren, Steve McQueen, Ingrid Bergman, The Beatles, and Coco Chanel appeared in and on covers of numerous international magazines, including *Life*, *Elle*,

nd *Paris Match*. After meeting in 1965, Sharon and Hatami formed
close bond. She came to look upon him as a confidante, and this
rust is supremely evident in the many photographs they created
ogether. Indeed, Hatami's studies of Sharon are unequivocally
reathtaking. Relaxed, unguarded, and often taken during private
noments without makeup or the trappings of designer couture, she
s somehow at her most tangible.

Sharon and fashion were strange bedfellows. She loved
designer clothing, and had impeccable taste, but was just as happy
n torn jeans and a T-shirt. She also had no hang-ups about being
naked, even before the camera. Indeed, with the sexual revolution
progressing she was the original "flower child." She wore nudity with
such comfort, with such innocence, that it immediately dissolved an
sense of the carnal and therefore made it seem okay to the most
austere observers.

Sharon was 5' 6" tall. She wore a size 6 dress (that's size 6 in
he 1960s, approximately size 2 in present time) and her shoe size
vas 6 1/2. Her personal style in terms of clothes was surprisingly
conservative. Sharon preferred clean, elegant, simple lines and su
n white or shades of ecru. She loved tailored clothing. Even her
peasant tops were tailored and she once had an Indian wedding
shirt custom-fit. She had blouses with hook and eye buttons mad
with spun gold. She particularly liked antique camisoles; wide belt

that could be worn over jeans or skirts; big hoop earrings and thin "love beads" that were made of tiny glass bugle beads. She was not big on rings or heavy necklaces. I think she didn't like rings because they brought attention to her hands and she used to bite her nails. Her favorite piece of jewelry was a Cartier watch with a black reptile band.

Despite the fact that Sharon entered stardom at the height of mod fashion's popularity, she rarely went in for extreme designs, saturated colors, and space-age synthetics. That said, she was a big fan of Rudi Gernreich and Betsey Johnson, and I once remember her wearing a Paco Rabanne "discotheque" top of aluminum pailettes. Needless to say she adored miniskirts and looked spectacular in them. She also loved Christian Dior, Pucci, Ossie Clark, as well as Chanel and Gucci handbags and shoes. Her favorite designer was Thea Porter, whose ethnic-inspired and richly embellished caftans and gypsy skirts made from silks, brocades, and velvets, were largely responsible for the late '60s revival in New Romanticism and the birth of the term "Hippy Chic."

The two of us loved to take our time walking and perusing the small boutiques on Melrose Avenue. This was where all the super-hip, up-and-coming designers were at the time—Twisted Sister, Rudi Gernreich, Grandpa Takes a Trip, etc. Betsey Johnson's store "Betsey Bunky Nini" was definitely the place to shop. Sharon particularly liked her knit dresses, pantsuits and A-line minis. We also ventured into Beverly Hills on occasion to visit Jax, a trendy department store owned by our friend Jack Hanson. Jack was quite famous in Los Angeles during that period as he also owned The Daisy, a notorious nightclub for Hollywood A-listers that had a $500 membership fee.

Designer boutiques aside, it was with Sharon that I invented a local fashion trend that many of our friends would borrow for years to come. It started during a hot summer in 1968. I had been laying by the pool while Sharon was giving Patty Duke's dog, Shadrack, a much needed bath on the lawn. Sharon and Roman had been renting Patty's house while she was in New York. Babysitting Shadrack, a beautiful Russian wolfhound, came as part of the deal. Unfortunately, the deal didn't include a fully stocked refrigerator, so famished (as usual) we each threw on a little shift dress, jumped into Sharon's white Rolls and ran down to Greenblatt's Delicatessen at the bottom of Laurel Canyon to pick up a couple of hot pastramis on rye. On arrival we were met at the door by a sign that read, "NO SHIRT. NO SHOES. NO SERVICE". We looked down at our bare feet, simultaneously sighed, and then headed back to the car. Suddenly I had a brainstorm. Earlier in the day we had gone to Rexall drugstore to pick up a few personal items for the house, including a ball of twine Sharon was going to use to rig a makeshift clothes line near the pool for wet bathing suits. I promptly measured an arm's length of twine and cut it with a pair of cuticle scissors Sis had in her purse. "What are you doing?" she asked incredulously. "Watch," I said as I took the twine, folded it in half, wrapped it around my big toe, crisscrossed it on top, wrapped it around my ankle, and then tied it in a bow at the back. The finished result gave the illusion that one was wearing a sandal. "What made you think of that?" Sharon asked in amazement. "HUNGER!" I replied. We both laughed as we finished dressing our feet and then went in and ordered our highly anticipated sandwiches. In time, we would come to call this invention "The Un-Shoe." We adored romping around the streets and trendy boutiques of L.A. in essentially bare feet. Eventually we improved on the idea by incorporating materials like colored ribbon and beads.

In her off time, when not working or being seen at a public event, Sharon was always freshly scrubbed, wore little or no makeup, and often kept her hair in a ponytail. She was not vain. It didn't matter to her if people saw her without makeup. Her favorite beauty product was simple Vaseline, for her lips. She would keep little jars in her car. She also liked Yardley clear lip gloss, and used her brown Max Factor eyebrow pencil as a lip liner. For skincare she preferred Erno Laszlo and she never went to bed with her makeup on. Sharon wasn't into perfume, as she was scent sensitive. Instead she made her own custom blend of essential oils, usually including tea rose. She also loved a bath product called "Milk and Pearls." I still have her last bottle.

The most beautiful

woman I ever met."

BERT STERN

"Sharon Tate is just dazzling. She evokes the sophistication and glamour of old Hollywood and the modest chic of today in one perfect package."

RICHARD AVEDON

Valley of the Dolls, 1967

"I have always considered Sharon Tate to be one of Hollywood's timeless beauties. Whether it be her hair, make-up or her designer clothing; Sharon's signature look from the '60s continues to influence designers and stylists as well as my own personal style on and off the red carpet."

KELLY OSBOURNE

Hatami, 1966. Dress by Mary Quant

"Even caught off-guard, Sharon was a study of elegance and poise."

DAVID BAILEY

ABOVE *Vogue*, April, 1966. Photos by David Bailey
RIGHT Photo by David Bailey, 1969

"She is shimmering blonde over high-cheekboned pale skin. She is a cascade of hair. She is lakewater hazel eyes. That thing of innocence. She is Sharon Tate, a name to remember, a talent to be reckoned with, a goddess who's got everything."

PHOTO SCREEN

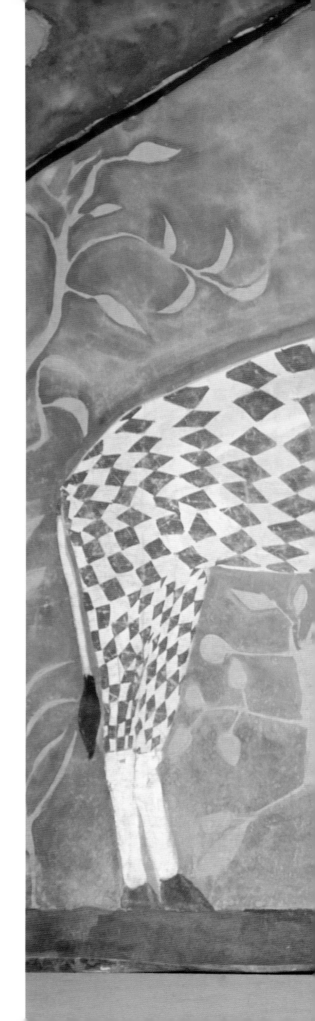

"I have never seen a woman who could stop traffic with her beauty like Sharon, and that in a town like Hollywood, known for its gorgeous girls!"

WARREN BEATTY

Milton Greene, 1966

"I'll always remember that day in spring when I met Sharon for the first time at the *Vogue* studio in Paris. In my career I have photographed the world's most attractive women, but Sharon is the one whose memory most deeply moves me. A charisma and an unforgettable beauty, she is still always on my mind."

JEAN-JACQUES BUGAT

Jean-Jacques Bugat, 1967

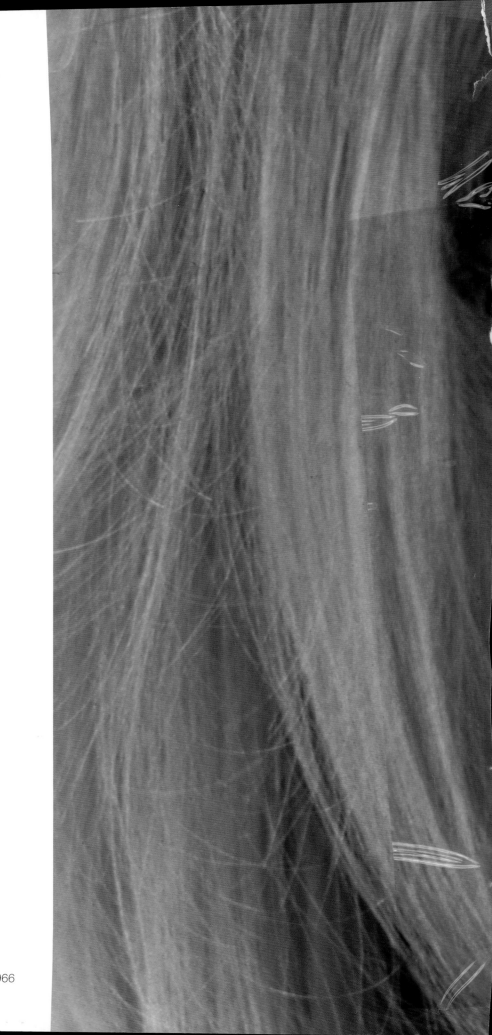

Orlando, 1966

"I remember the photo shoot with Sharon Tate very well. It was for an article on fur coats in *Harper's Bazaar*. The hat she is wearing was designed by Halston. We just got in the car and drove up to Central Park. The art director suggested the back of a car, and I thought up the idea using dogs and the chauffer. It just made it more interesting. Sharon was friendly, sweet, and very charming, quite physical as well. She liked to touch and I remember her once putting her hand on my knee, in a purely innocent way. She did her makeup herself and was brilliant in front of the camera. Very exotic and a delight to work with."

NEAL BARR

Neal Barr, *Harper's Bazaar*, 1967. Hat by Halston

"Sharon was so amazingly down to earth, her ethereal beauty seemed to captivate all those around her, but she seemed oblivious to it and the effect she had on strangers. She would sometimes flirt a bit, but it was well known around Hollywood that Sharon was a one-man girl, and she kept true to herself and never slept around. A rare thing in young actresses trying to get their 'big break,' I can tell you. There was something very 'special' about her and we were very protective of her too."

KIRK DOUGLAS

Peter Basch, 1965. Red fox mini coat by JAX of Beverly Hills

"Sharon Tate has transcended her career in the '60s to become one of the great fashion and style icons of the twentieth century and beyond. A designer's dream, and one of the few actresses of her time to blur the line between movie star and fashion model in the pages of *Vogue* and *Bazaar*, she looked equally as dynamic in haute couture as she did in a bikini. Whether it was Christian Dior, Pucci, Ossie Clark, the mod fashions of Rudi Gernreich and Betsey Johnson, the 'hippy chic' of Thea Porter (her favorite designer), or the glitzy 'Hollywood' creations of Travilla for *Valley of the Dolls*, Sharon Tate's style, signature eye makeup, and cascading blonde hair are today constantly referenced on the runway, the red carpet, and in magazine editorials worldwide. In 2013 Mattel produced their second Malibu Barbie doll—'Malibu Barbie by Trina Turk.' The original Malibu Barbie from 1971 was actually inspired by Sharon's character, 'Malibu' in the MGM film *Don't Make Waves*."

TRINA TURK (Designer)

"Sharon Tate, in so many different attitudes and poses was always a delight to work with and very professional. She worked hard to get the right shot and was a lot of fun always."

JOHN ENGSTEAD

John Engstead, 1964

"Sharon was more than just stunning to look at. She wasn't naive or stupid or a cliché starlet. What had impressed me most about her, quite apart from her exceptional beauty, was the sort of radiance that springs from a kind and gentle nature; she had obvious hang-ups yet seemed completely liberated. I'd never met anyone like her before."

ROMAN POLANSKI

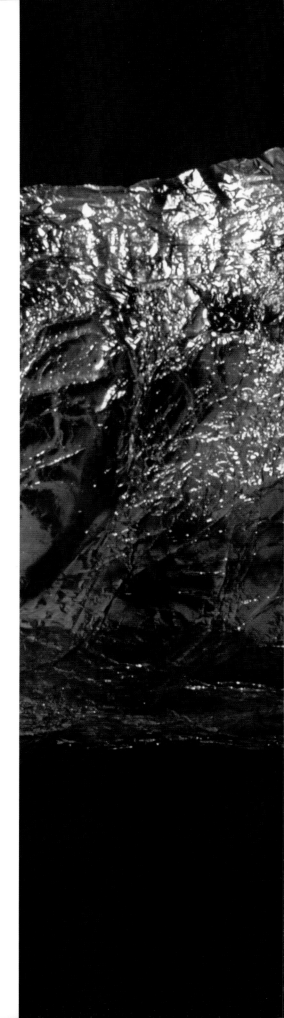

Hatami, 1969

"I'd like to be a fairy princess—a little golden doll with gossamer wings, in a voile dress, adorned with bright, shiny things. I see that as something totally pure and beautiful. Everything that's realistic has some sort of ugliness in it. Even a flower is ugly when it wilts, a bird when it seeks its prey, the ocean when it becomes violent. I'm very sensitive to ugly situations. I'm quick to read people, and I pick up if someone's reacting to me as just a sexy blonde. At times like that, I freeze. I can be very alone at a party, on the set, or in general, if I'm not in harmony with things around me."

SHARON TATE

Philippe Halsman, 1966

Roman

Shalazar

It was in the early fall of 1967. Sharon called to announce that she was bringing her new fiancé home to meet the family. Sis had spoken about Roman so enthusiastically during the filming of *The Fearless Vampire Killers* in France, that we knew this relationship was something special. We were familiar with the name Roman Polanski, as he had already made an indelible impression on the world of cinema, but the man himself was yet to be introduced. We were all in a tizzy, especially Mom, who was throwing orders for the final spit shining of the already perfectly clean three-story Victorian house we had come to call home. Fort Baker, one of the few military bases we ever lived on, was most unusual. The pre-World War I installation was perched on some of the world's most valuable real estate overlooking the Golden Gate Bridge—with the San Francisco Bay on one side and the Pacific Ocean on the other. It had grand oak trees and rolling hills of lush, green grass on the northern side spotted with grazing cattle. I was never happier than when I lived there.

Sharon had bought me a two-year-old filly to keep me busy while she was working abroad. I named her Shalazar. She was an extraordinary light blonde color with a thick, black mane and tail, and being half Arabian she had a beautiful head. I was in love with this animal and couldn't wait to show her off to Sharon and Roman. The pair had driven up to the North Bay and checked into the grand old Sausalito Inn, a historical landmark that had been a whorehouse in the 1800s. It had a charming and romantic atmosphere. I found my way off the base and into town to meet up with the pair prior to the rest of the family. On arrival, I was invited up to the room to put a very nervous Roman at ease. I think he thought we were going to eat him for supper. We instantly bonded after a stream of jokes on the subject and a long laugh.

My first impression of Roman was that he didn't quite look the same in person as he did in the photographs I had seen. While he was certainly handsome in a manly way, there was a cute "puppy" quality to him that was absolutely adorable. I could see why Sis was so enamored. Sharon wanted my opinion on nice restaurants in the area as she and Roman were planning a formal dinner to take place the following evening. We walked to view two of my suggestions, Ondine and The Trident, to see if they would be suitable. Roman chose Ondine for its world-class French cuisine and spectacular view of the bay. I didn't know it at the time, but his intention was to ask Sharon for her hand in marriage (a second time) at the restaurant, so the family could be included.

On the way back to the base, I wanted to make a brief detour and show Sis the horse she had given me, but she said we would do that after lunch. I was slightly disappointed but later understood that we needed to make haste for Roman's nerve to stay strong. We arrived at the house and Mom and Patti came running out to greet us. Dad, forever the sly old fox, came swaggering out last, so he had time to size Roman up as he was meeting the others. I could see why Roman was so apprehensive earlier as Dad's attitude and body language was very foreboding. Dad must have liked what he saw though, because he extended his hand in an approving manner and invited us all into the house for lunch. There was a lot of table conversation as everyone got to know one another. Roman seemed very comfortable and I could see that he had found his own spot as a soon-to-be member of our family.

My time came—and none too soon—when we all went back toward town and stopped on the way to see my Shalazar. Mom and Patti stood at the fence as Dad and I entered the large enclosure we had built specially for her. Sharon and Roman followed, paused, and then Roman asked if it was safe. "Oh, yes," I assured him, "I've done a lot of work with Shalazar. Would you like to ride her as well?" Before Sharon could object, Roman replied with a confident "yes," so I promptly caught Shalazar, put a halter on her, and then urged both of them to touch and speak to her as we prepared. Roman, wanting to be the man, went first. Dad and I got him on board awkwardly, and I then urged Sharon to walk her slowly around the enclosure. Shalazar began to canter and all of a sudden we heard a desperate, "OH NO!!! . . . I DON'T!!! . . . OH NO, SHE'S LOSING ME!!!" Just the way he said it made everyone break out laughing. And Sharon laughed the hardest. You see, only Roman could exercise such verbal control in an uncontrollable situation.

ABOVE With Roman, Sharon, and Shalazar. Sausalito, 1967 **OVERLEAF** Sharon visiting the set of Roman's film *Rosemary's Baby*. The Dakota, New York, August 28, 1967. Photo by Santi Visalli

London Airport, January 1967. Note Sharon's dog carrier containing her beloved Yorkie, Sapirstein.

"They were the Douglas Fairbanks and Mary Pickford of our time.… cool, nomadic, talented and nicely shocking. Their 'Pickfair' was a movable mansion, a roomy rebellion. Curious, unafraid, they helped demolish the ancient Hollywood image of what movie stardom was all about. They became part of the 'anti-establishment' establishment. They became rich but never regal."

PETER EVANS

"He's very sympathetic, very sensitive, very intelligent and a combination of explosives. You don't notice any one part of Roman—he comes at you in one dynamic blast! Roman is such a beautiful, mad human being. Sometimes things are difficult, sometimes good, but it makes life twice as interesting. He's wise, wonderful and brilliant and he knows everything. Roman has helped me to grow tremendously, it's about time wouldn't you say?! Because of him and his acting business, I'm starting to see things for what they're worth. Because I used to take everything at face value. Because when I say something I mean it…. so I used to feel that everybody else meant what they said, but of course that wasn't true and life isn't that sweet and simple. I guess I kind of lived in a fairytale…looking at everything through rose-colored glasses, I probably always will to a certain extent."

SHARON TATE

"Sharon was one of the most beautiful brides I had ever seen at her wedding to Roman in 1968. It was at the Playboy Club in London, then at the height of its louche popularity. Sharon looked ravishing— her long blonde hair was done in intricate coils, and laced with 'baby's breath.' I too had a complicated hairdo of the times and we had a sweet picture together in which we laughingly compared our 'do's.' Roman in his Beatles jacket looked like the cat that found the cream. It was a fabulous wedding and everyone had a fabulous time."

JOAN COLLINS

OPPOSITE Sharon and Roman on their wedding day at the Chelsea registry office. London, January 20, 1968. Dress by Alba.
ABOVE With Joan Collins at the wedding reception. Playboy Club, London, January 20, 1968

"The wedding ceremony turned into a media event with photographers outnumbering the guests. Sharon wore a cream colored taffeta minidress and I sported an olive green Edwardian jacket. There were several parties afterwards, the biggest of them all, at the Playboy Club, was attended by what seemed like the whole of London and half of Hollywood. Halfway through the festivities Sharon and I bowed out, we couldn't take anymore parties or champagne so we headed for West Eaton Place Mews and holed up in our house, which was littered with gifts, flowers, and congratulatory telegrams."

ROMAN POLANSKI

Opening gifts at West Eaton Place Mews. London, January 20, 1968

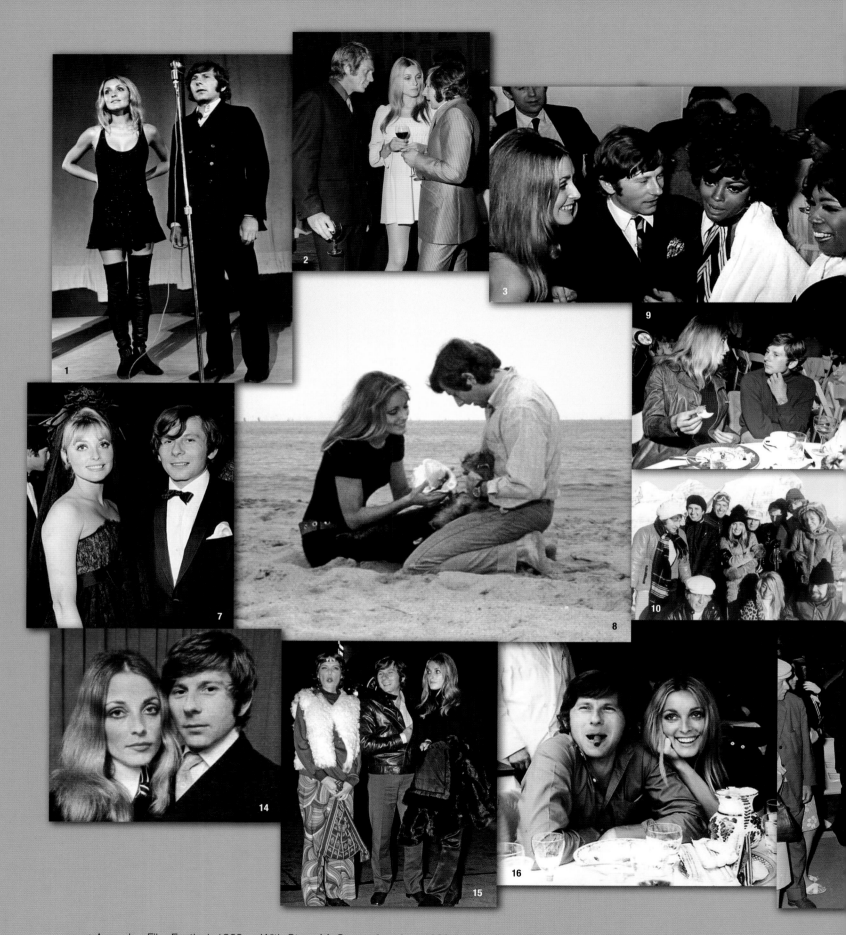

1 Acapulco Film Festival, 1968   **2** With Steve McQueen, London, 1969   **3** With Diana Ross and Mary Wilson   **4** With Hugh Hefner on *Playboy After Dark*, 1969   **5** Visiting Federico Fellini during filming of *Fellini Satyricon*, 1969   **6** At the London premiere of *Rosemary's Baby*, January 24, 1969. Snakeskin coat by Ossie Clark   **7** At the London premiere of *Cul-de-Sac*, 1966. Dress by Dior   **8** c. 1968

9 Photo by Nate Cutler 10 Honeymoon in Gstaad, 1968 11 Cannes, May 1968 12 c. 1968 13 Chateau Marmont, L.A., 1968 14 London, 1968. Photo by John Kelly. Dress by Ossie Clark 15 With Mia Farrow, Los Angeles 16 Cannes, May 1968. Photo by Elio Sorci 17 Cannes Film Festival, 1968 18 With Jane Fonda at the premiere of *Goodbye Columbus*, Los Angeles, March 1969 19 Cannes Film Festival, May 1968

"Just about the only really happily married couple I knew in Hollywood were Roman Polanski and Sharon Tate. Coming from a childhood of horror in Nazi-occupied Poland, Roman couldn't believe he was the husband of this milk-fed American beauty....In Roman's eyes, she was already the brightest star in the world. Around his gentle, sun-kissed bride he was like a child who's just seen his first Christmas tree light up."

ROBERT EVANS

ABOVE Sharon and Roman arrive at the Golden Globe Awards. The Ambassador Hotel, February 12, 1968. Sharon was nominated that evening as Most Promising Female Newcomer for *Valley of the Dolls.* OPPOSITE The Golden Globe Awards, 1968

Cannes, May 1968. Photo by Jack Garofalo

"She was a unique person. It's difficult to describe her character. She was just utterly good, the kindest human being I've ever met, with an extreme patience. To live with me was proof of her patience, because to be near me must be an ordeal. She never had a bad temper, she was never moody. She enjoyed being a wife. The press and the public knew of her physical beauty, but she also had a beautiful soul, and this is something that only her friends knew about."

ROMAN POLANSKI

"What enchanted me about her as much as anything was her immutable good nature, her high spirits, her love of people and animals—of life itself. Over-demonstrative, over-solicitous women had always made me uneasy, but Sharon struck the perfect balance between affection and concern. Though more a spectator than a participant in our gags and shenanigans, she had a great sense of humour. She was also a born housewife. Aside from cooking like a dream, she used to cut my hair, a skill acquired from Jay Sebring. She liked to pack my bag whenever I had to take a trip. She always knew exactly what to put in—so much so that I can never pack or unpack, even today, without thinking of her."

ROMAN POLANSKI

ABOVE Cannes, May 1968. Photo by Jack Garofalo. Minidress by Lord Kitcheners of London **OVERLEAF** On the town, 1969   225

"There are little things, like packing a suitcase or getting my hair cut or dialing the 213 code for California or the 396 code for Rome, that invariably steer my thoughts back to Sharon. Even after so many years I find myself unable to watch a spectacular sunset or visit a lovely old house or experience visual pleasure of any kind without instinctively telling myself how much she would have loved it all. In these ways I shall remain faithful to her till the day I die."

ROMAN POLANSKI

London, 1968. Photo by Terry O'Neill

Nova

1968

"She was a very, very gentle person. Very gentle. Very much a flower power child. But not silly. She was very cool. Jeans looked very good on her. And she was the first one that wore a see-through top, but it worked, you know, it was ok."

BRIAN MORRIS

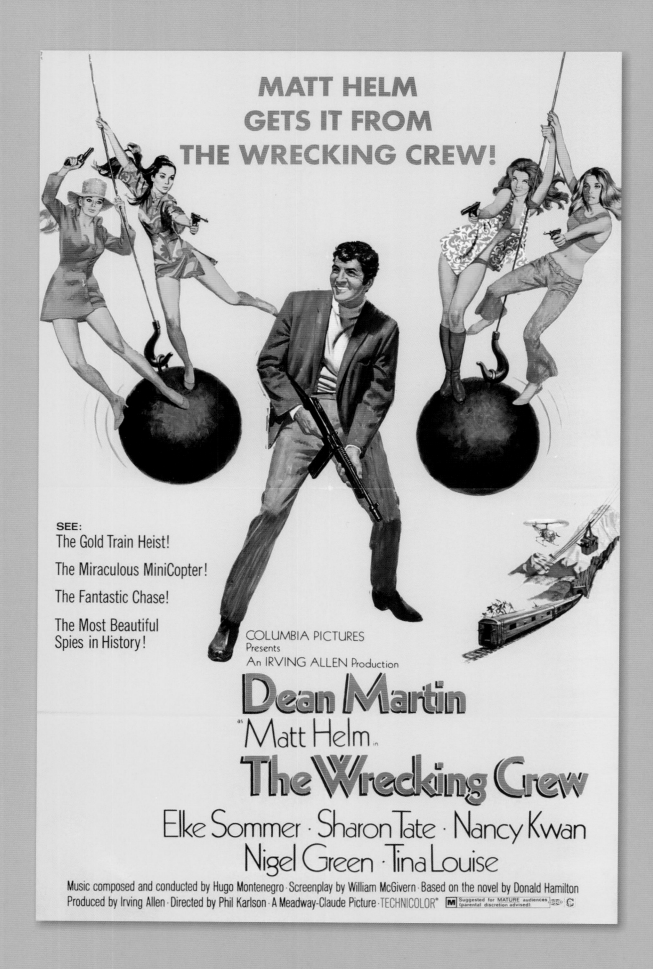

"Sharon Tate reveals a pleasant affinity to scatterbrain comedy and comes as close to walking away with this picture as she did in a radically different role in *Valley of the Dolls*."

THE HOLLYWOOD REPORTER

ABOVE Sharon on set with Dean Martin, *The Wrecking Crew*, 1968.

"Always sultry, always sexy, always classy. Sharon had style and grace."

DEAN MARTIN

ABOVE Sharon (as Freya Carlson) with Dean Martin (as Matt Helm), *The Wrecking Crew*, 1968 **OPPOSITE** *The Wrecking Crew.* Nannie Tate was so enamored with Sharon's baby blue and white striped cap in the film that following production Sharon acquired it and presented it to Nannie as a gift.

The Master — Bruce Lee, 1968

I was never able to visit the set of Sharon's movie *The Wrecking Crew* as our family was still living in Sausalito at that time and I was in school. Mom and Dad were proud as punch that their daughter would be starring opposite Dean Martin in the fourth (and final) film in the popular Matt Helm series. Most exciting of all was the fact that in preparation for her role, Sharon was being trained by *the* Kung Fu Master, Bruce Lee.

A few years back, when Sharon was dating Jay Sebring, we went to watch Jay train with his friend Master Lee on numerous occasions. At the time, Sharon never had much interaction with Bruce beyond an introduction, hellos, and goodbyes. Now she was working with him herself. While on spring break from school, I remember weeks of Sharon's one-on-one training with Master Lee. I was always invited to join in the workout. Many times we would rendezvous at the Chuck Norris Studio on Santa Monica Boulevard in West Los Angeles. I learned so much from Master Lee, but the thing I remember most is what a wonderful, kind, passionate, and incredibly funny man he was. Sometimes to break the tension in the room when Sharon was having trouble achieving her assigned move, Bruce would call on me saying, "Come on little wild thing. Shall we show her how it's done?" and he and I would do the routine together. I, of course, couldn't perform without making the classic kung fu sound effects. This always cracked Sharon up, and then we would all start laughing. Many times after this experience, during frustrating moments, either Sharon or I would spontaneously break into a chorus of "Wild Thing" to ease the tension. It still makes me smile.

Sharon on set with Bruce Lee, Nancy Kwan, and director Phil Karlson, *The Wrecking Crew*, 1968.

"By the time you get to the point where you have the power to run your own career, they call you a bitch."

SHARON TATE

The Wrecking Crew, 1968

"She was the most beautiful woman I ever saw. Spontaneous and wickedly funny."

STEVE MCQUEEN

"During the shooting of the movie *The Wrecking Crew*, Sharon and I grew very close, almost like sisters. As I am an only child, this was a completely new experience for me. Sharon gave me her trust and her friendship and she introduced me to the music of Leonard Cohen—three 'things' that made my life richer, better, and brighter."

ELKE SOMMER

ABOVE With Elke Sommer (as Linka Karensky), *The Wrecking Crew*

1968: **1** Summitridge Drive **2** With Julie Christie and Warren Beatty at the Los Angeles premiere of *Rosemary's Baby* **3** Los Angeles **4** With Truman Capote in Cannes **5** Summitridge Drive. Photo by Alan Pappé **6** With Kirk Douglas at the premiere of *The Legend of Lylah Clare,* the Troubadour **7** With director Louis Malle **8** Washing Patty Duke's dog Shadrack at Summitridge Drive **9** With Richard Gregson and Natalie Wood at The Golden Globe Awards. The Ambassador Hotel, February 12, 1968

At the premiere of *Rosemary's Baby*, Cannes Film Festival, May 1968

1969

"Ah, Sharon. The word 'exquisite' perfectly sums up this lady. Almost otherworldly, so beautiful and sensitive, a truly gentle soul. But in no way wishy-washy, she was smart and not taken in by the shallowness of the industry. Well-grounded and natural, she was very much in tune with her life and really happy when I last saw her in London in 1969. She was such an innocent, and unspoiled by her success."

GEORGE HARRISON

Photos by Peter Brüchmann

I met Sharon Tate in 1969 at the Malibu Colony cottage of Jane Fonda and Roger Vadim. Jane had phoned while I was having a massage on the set of *Lions Love* to tell me she had just seen Warhol's *Lonesome Cowboys* and was a huge fan. This was at a time when independent cinema was beginning to make a big impact in Hollywood.

She invited me and Michel Auder, whom I later married, to dinner. When we arrived everyone was already eating. The only other guests were Sharon and her husband, Roman Polanski. At the head of the table Jane was wearing a priest's chasuble in green and gold, symbolizing hope and new growth. Sharon offered me a Coke out of the fridge and I took my place at the other end of the table. I marveled at the way the burning candles lit up the gold in Jane's *They Shoot Horses, Don't They* hairdo and the embroidery on the chasuble which glittered every time she made the slightest move. She was clearly the archbishop of the beach.

Sharon sat demurely to my left, hugely pregnant, breasts bursting from her decolletage, her skin luminously radiant, her eyes huge. She was extraordinarily beautiful, unearthly looking even—you just couldn't take your eyes off her. She seemed happy singing along to Leonard Cohen's "Suzanne" playing in the background.

VIVA

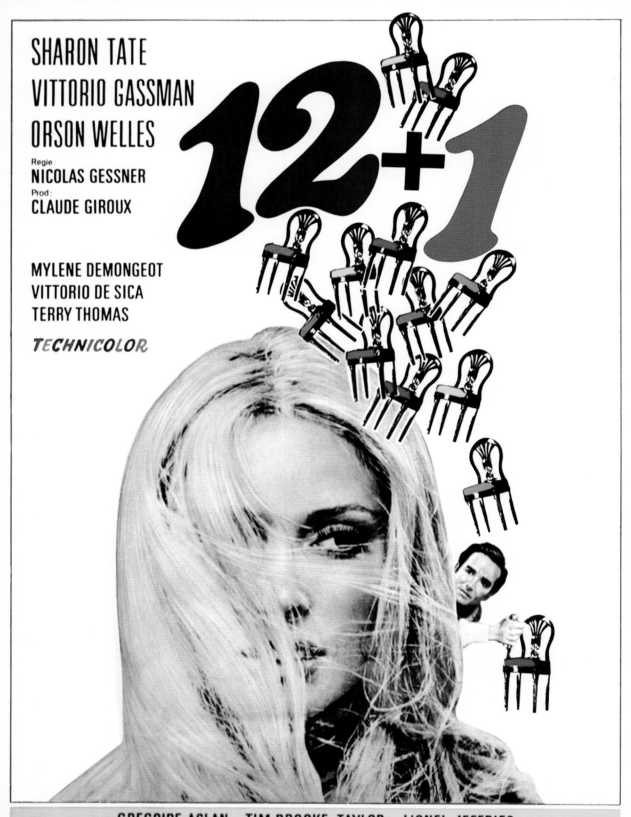

254

"I am a big fan of her still. I was convinced that with her talents she would have been a really big, BIG star. I think objectively, she had this very rare, unique quality. As François Truffaut would say, 'The camera loved her!'"

NICOLAS GESSNER (Director)

"Sublime . . . exquisitely elegant."

ORSON WELLES

ABOVE Sharon (as Pat) with Vittorio Gassman (as Mario Beretti), *12 + 1*, 1969 OPPOSITE *12 + 1*, 1969

"In Europe, everything is so much more liberal and open. So much more realistic. The whole freedom outlook over there is just fantastic. People aren't worried about what society is going to think—as long as the feelings are there…and the feelings are honest. Men in Europe cry and in airports they kiss their sons right on the lips, emotion makes them real men."

SHARON TATE

ABOVE Rome, 1969

12 + 1, 1969.
Photos by Terry O'Neill

Can I describe Sharon?

It is unimaginable that I'd be asked to do so.

Beautiful, of course, the kind that would glide into a room—not walk. Playful and funny, sweet and tender, gracious and warm-hearted.

She had haute couture hippy meets *Vogue* and *Harper's* style, and the gorgeous body to wear Damascus brocades, Chinese silks, Indian saris, or nothing at all. A modern Goddess.

When we were in London she told me she was pregnant but that Roman didn't know yet, and with that sweet mischievous smile on her face said she wanted to smoke one last cigarette before telling him that night.

She was the gracious hostess who included anyone she might find charming regardless of status. She was adoring and adored.

Back in Los Angeles she showed me swaths of wallpaper for the nursery—difficult to do, not knowing the sex of the baby. In that flowing paisley chiffon dress she floated in blissful readiness. Her wide, bright eyes shining with happiness.

That is what she is—always and forever—a euphoric, radiant soul, a mythical creature who comes to me in my dreams and in all our joyful, elated, and gleeful moments.

That's Sharon.

MICHELLE PHILLIPS

Photo by Hatami, 1969. Caftan designed by Thea Porter

The Moon Landing

1969 ended the decade with a bang. Indeed, the '60s had unleashed an avalanche of change that marked the birth of contemporary culture. In 1969, the Vietnam War remained a ceaseless global tragedy that politically divided the country. Civil rights unrest continued to incite the cause. Richard Nixon became our thirty-seventh president. Woodstock united us for three days of peace and music. And the Stonewall riots in New York City marked the start of the modern gay rights movement. We said goodbye to Judy Garland and Brian Jones of the Rolling Stones, and hello to the Concorde and Wal-Mart. Golda Meir became the first female prime minister of Israel. And a Missouri teenager died of a baffling medical condition later identified as AIDS.

It was a confusing time for a girl. I had entered my teenage years in an era of Kennedy puritanism. Suddenly around 1965 everything changed. The world was asking questions and, not always happy with the answers, decided to explore and seek its own truth. At first the results were promising—the counterculture; free love; philosophy and the new ways of thinking; the embracing of Eastern religions; women's liberation and the progression of the sexual revolution; all pointed towards a society in search of a better way. Unfortunately, at the same time, these good intentions were being fueled by an increasingly rampant combination of heroin, LSD, and amphetamines. In the end, by 1969, everything the decade had promised came crashing down and ultimately culminated in a generation of confused youth and a society in moral decay.

But then, in a respite from the darkness, there was the moon landing. The entire world had been waiting in anticipation for this monumental achievement—"one giant leap for mankind"—which was to take place on July 20. We had come down from Sausalito, as school was out and we had begun the process of moving back to southern California. Sharon was back home after finishing her film *12 + 1*, and the whole family would bare witness to this historic event together.

Sharon greeted us as we walked up the path towards the house. She was wearing a bikini bottom and a simple top that I had made for her. I was delighted to see her wearing it. Her very pregnant belly peeked out just slightly between the two pieces of clothing. I was the first one to reach the porch. I held out my hand and touched her belly as I bent down to greet the baby, then stood up and greeted my sister. Patti, who was dragging a plethora of pool toys, followed suit. Mom was next, and then Dad pulled up the rear with his signature cigar clenched firmly between his teeth, his arms overflowing with all the goodies Mom had prepared. These included a ham and fried chicken, which Sis had specially requested. I ran back to the car for the potato salad and baked beans and my personal gift for Sharon and baby—a tractor inner tube big enough for her midsection to fit through. This way she could float comfortably and allow her belly to become weightless. She said she couldn't wait to try it out. We quickly set up the buffet on the dining room table and jumped in the pool, where we spent a good portion of the day laughing, splashing, talking, and eating. It really was a glorious afternoon.

Dad came out of the house and announced it was time. The television broadcast of the moon landing was about to start. We all got out of the pool, put on dry clothes, and piled on the bed to watch this unbelievable event unfold. As Apollo 11 settled itself onto the lunar surface, there was a feeling of global unity so palpable that I almost couldn't hold back my tears. For that brief moment we seemed at peace. I couldn't help but think about all of the ways our lives were about to change, both personally and as a nation. Mom had said that because of the moon landing the world would advance in so many wonderful ways. With this in the forefront of our minds, we all got off the bed and went to the kitchen to clean the dishes, pack up, and ready ourselves for the trip home.

Mom, slightly emotional as mothers often are when leaving their children, asked Sis if she was going to be all right and if there was anything she might need. Sharon assured her, "No, silly. I'm okay. I have everything I need," as her eyes glanced down towards her belly. We all filed out of the house, Sharon behind us. She waited for us to get in the car to start waving goodbye, and we all did the same until we exited the large gate.

I looked over my shoulder to wave one last time and noticed her standing in the doorway. She resembled Botticelli's Venus with her hand under her belly and her corn-colored hair dancing gently in the breeze. She became smaller and smaller as we rounded the corner until, finally, she disappeared.

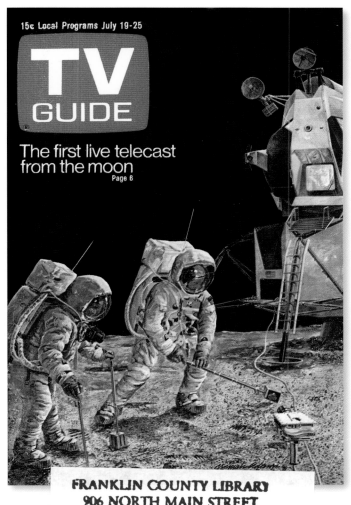

ABOVE AND OPPOSITE Sharon and I. Los Angeles, July, 1969. In the photos at top, I'm wearing one of Sharon's dresses—this one designed by Joan Arkin.

Photo Credits

20th Century Fox Photo Archive – *Valley of the Dolls* © 1967 Twentieth Century Fox. All Rights Reserved
Pages: 139, 142-143, 148, 149, 150, 154, 155, 170-171

Andrew Hansford / The Estate of William Travilla
Page: 144 (top left, top right, bottom right)

Corbis
Pages: 186-187

David Bailey / Camera Eye Ltd. / © David Bailey
Pages: 174-175

David Wills
Pages: 65, 74, 84, 97, 98, 105, 106, 108, 114, 120, 122, 134, 135 (20th Century Fox), 156 (left), 234, 254, 267

Getty Images
Pages: 90, 95, 184-185, 208-209, 222, 225, 228-229, 260-261

Globe Photos / Image Collect
Page: 218

Independent Visions
Pages: Cover, 60, 63, 85, 102, 116, 124-125 (20th Century Fox), 152, 182-183, 197, 215, 218, 220, 221, 246

Jean-Jacques Bugat (jeanjacquesbugat.com)
Pages: 180-181

Magnum Photos / Philippe Halsman
Pages: 160-161, 201

Margaret Herrick Library / The Academy of Motion Picture Arts and Sciences
Pages: 81, 146 (20th Century Fox)

Milton H. Greene. Photographed by Milton H. Greene © 2013 Joshua Greene (www.archiveimages.com)
Pages: 176-177, 178-179

MPTV (mptvimages.com)
Page: 137

Neal Barr (nealbarr.com)
Pages: 190-191

Peter Brüchmann / Grauwert Digital Fine Art (grauwert.de)
Pages: 250, 251, 252

Photofest (photofestnyc.com)
Pages: 1, 6, 47, 52, 53, 54, 55, 92, 93, 101, 107, 126 (20th Century Fox), 140, 141, 144 (bottom left), 147 (20th Century Fox), 153 (20th Century Fox), 189, 192-193, 202-203, 210, 214, 217, 218, 219, 230-231, 239, 245, 246, 247, 272. The Christopher Simmons Collection – Pages: 58, 59, 66-67, 68-69, 76-77, 83, 91 (right), 100, 110, 113, 156 (right), 157, 158, 159, 194, 213, 218, 219, 233, 235, 240, 241, 242, 243, 244, 256, 257, 259. The Andrea Wagner Collection – Pages: 61, 91 (left), 123, 158, 159, 218, 246. The Muriel Colson-Wagner Collection – Pages: 111, 158, 159, 198-199, 219, 236, 237, 248-249, 263, 246

Rex USA
Pages: 57, 64, 86, 89, 121, 172

The Kobal Collection (picture-desk.com)
Pages: 78, 79, 82, 96, 117, 118, 226-227

The Tate Family Archive
Pages: 10-11, 12, 13, 14, 16, 17, 18, 19, 20, 21, 22, 23, 26, 27, 28, 29, 32, 33, 34, 35, 36-37, 38, 40, 41, 44, 45, 46, 48-49, 50, 73, 88, 103, 119, 207, 268, 269